MW00996438

AVENGERS CAMPUS

THE OFFICIAL COOKBOOK

JENNIFER FUJIKAWA + MARC SUMERAK

INSIGHT EDITIONS
San Rafael · Los Angeles · London

PYM
TECHNOLOGIES
Goliath

PYM
TECHNOLOGIES
PYM
TECHNOLOGIES

CONTENTS

V = Vegetarian

V+ = Vegan

GF = Gluten-Free

INTRODUCTION

HEY, YOU GUYS! You are SO not going to believe what I did this summer . . . I SOLVED WORLD HUNGER!!!

Okay, maybe that's a bit of an exaggeration. I mean, it's still all hypothetical. At least for now. But my dad says I'm definitely onto something big. And if anyone knows BIG, it's him, so, you know . . .

Wait. Maybe you don't know! I should probably rewind a bit before my excitement gets the best of me. Which it does. A lot. Especially when I talk about all the cool stuff I've been working on.

My name is Cassie Lang. You might not know me (yet!), but you've probably seen my dad, Scott, off saving the world alongside the Avengers as the astonishing Ant-Man. But there's also a solid chance you've never seen him at all, because he gets, like, really, really tiny. Then again, other times, he gets insanely huge. That's kind of his thing. But technically, it's not actually his thing . . . Hang on, let me explain.

See, my dad got his powers from this legendary scientist named Dr. Henry Pym (we just call him Hank). A long time ago, Hank discovered these revolutionary particles that—well, there's a super-scientific explanation to them that requires an in-depth understanding of quantum theory—but basically, they make things shrink or grow. He named them "Pym Particles," because . . . you know what? I'm pretty sure you can figure out that part by yourself.

Anyway, my dad—let's say "borrowed"—one of Dr. Pym's size-changing suits to become Ant-Man. He went on some crazy adventures, joined the Avengers, and teamed up with Hank's daughter, Hope van Dyne—who is, like, one of the coolest and smartest people I have ever met in my entire life! Hope eventually got a super-suit of her own and became the wonderful Wasp. Basically, she's like Ant-Man but with wings and energy blasters. Oh, and she's also my hero. (Don't worry. My dad knows . . . and he totally agrees!)

While Dad and Hope typically use their size-altering abilities to kick bad guys in the butt, I found myself wondering how Pym Particles could be applied to make the everyday world a better place. Or at least that's what I always tell everyone in interviews. To be honest, I was actually just daydreaming about my dad enlarging a sprinkle donut to the size of an SUV. But that's when it hit me: If food were BIGGER, it would feed a lot more people!

It seems like such an obvious idea, right? Makes you wonder how no one ever thought of it before me. But let's be fair. Heroes are always so busy fending off alien attacks and whatever else that they never really have the time to stop and think about the other ways that their powers could benefit the rest of us. And I don't blame them. If Thanos was punching me in the face, I'd probably be focused on fighting him, not famine.

So, I decided to draw out my idea for a school project, focusing on how Pym Particles could both increase food supplies and reduce waste. It got an A, which is great. But more importantly, it also got Hope's attention. She realized there was something special about my idea and decided to open a brand-new branch of Pym Technologies devoted entirely to food science! You have no idea how it feels when something you did inspires the person who inspires you. Or maybe you do. I really hope so, because it feels totally awesome!

Hope and her research team opened up the Pym Test Kitchen to start the Research & Development (or, R&D) process, experimenting with phenomenal foods at unusual scales. Not only that, they also started looking for ways that Pym Particles could decrease the environmental footprint of traditional food production methods. As they like to say, "Small actions on the plate mean big impacts for a healthy planet." (It's a pretty clever slogan. I wish I had come up with it myself.) And while I'm still a bit too young to officially join their team, it wasn't long before I found myself on an adventure of my own . . . right next door!

Turns out, the same idea that inspired the Pym Test Kitchen also caught the attention of the folks at the Worldwide Engineering Brigade—or WEB, as us cool kids like to call it. It's basically a think tank of up-and-coming young inventors and visionaries from all over the world, brought to you by the fine folks at Stark Industries. (I have to say that last part. It's in the contract. But they really are great, I swear!)

And that's how I ended up spending my summer on the Avengers Campus, working at the WEB Workshop alongside the next generation of big brains as we dreamed up innovative new ways to save the world without ever throwing a punch. But while we each had our own special projects to lead (mine involved unorthodox applications of Pym Particles, obviously!), we were all more than willing to serve as the primary test subjects for the edible experiments coming out of the Pym Test Kitchen.

Which brings me to why I'm writing this book. See, now that the summer is over, I have to head back to the Bay Area to stay with my mom and her husband, Jim.

I love it there, don't get me wrong. But I'm really going to miss my new friends, not to mention all of the itty-bitty burgers and supersized snacks available at the Avengers Campus. That's why I convinced Hope to let me gather some of her team's favorite formulas for me to try to make at home. I've even discovered a bunch of new recipes not featured at Avengers Campus that my friends and I wanted to share with you.

From big bites to microscopic meals, hopefully these R&D recipes will recapture the magic of life on campus and remind me of what it feels like to be part of something superspecial. And I'm sharing them with you (after getting all of the proper clearances from the Pym Technologies legal team, of course) because I bet you could use some extra adventure added into your daily dining as well!

There's a good chance that these experimental eats won't always turn out exactly as they would've if they'd been made in the Test Kitchen (especially the brand-new recipes, just for this cookbook)—unless you managed to get your hands on a stash of Pym Particles somehow. But that's kind of what science is all about, right? Part of the fun is finding out what your final results are going to be! And you don't need to worry . . . the chances that any of these formulas end up shrinking you into the Quantum Realm are really, really slim. (Like 5 percent at most.) P.S.—If there's one thing that all of the best scientists and chefs I've met have in common, it's this: They take tons of notes! So I made sure to leave you some extra pages in the back where you can jot down your favorite meal combos, ingredient substitution ideas, or complex chemical equations. Whatever comes to mind. It's your space. Do what works for you!

So, there you have it. I dreamed big so that you could eat bigger (or in some cases, much, much smaller). Maybe I haven't completely solved world hunger quite yet, but with some help, I've taken a step in the right direction. And when you're part of my family, a single step can take you pretty far. Give some of this cutting-edge cuisine a try and I bet it won't be long before you come to the same conclusion I did: All it takes are some fresh ingredients and some even fresher ideas to change the world . . . one meal at a time!

Enjoy!

CASSIE

BLUE Pym Particles
+ existing food → feed
more people & have
GIANT SNACKS
= WIN/WIN
-SCOTT

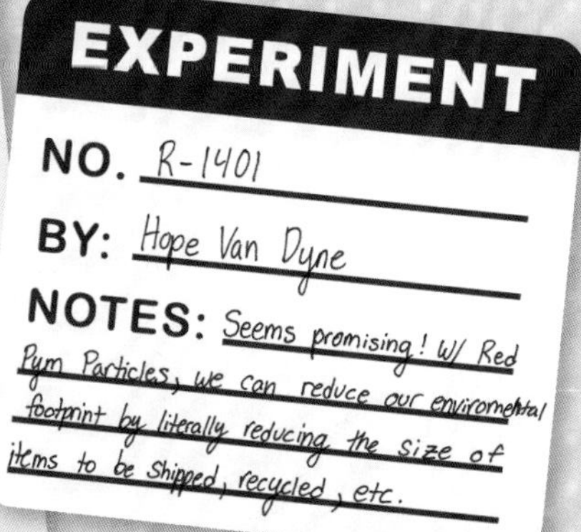

EXPERIMENT
NO. R-1401
BY: Hope Van Dyne
NOTES: Seems promising! W/ Red Pym Particles, we can reduce our environmental footprint by literally reducing the size of items to be shipped, recycled, etc.

Name: Cassie Lang
Grade: 7
Illustrate how science could make the world better.
How To FEED the WORLD
With Pym Tech!
X
10X
PYM DISK
BLUE = Big
RED = Reduce

Note: Some of the recipes included in this book are not available at Avengers Campus or Disney California Adventure.

PYM
TEST KITCHEN

CHAPTER 1

SIZED TO SHARE

APPETIZERS

To be honest, before I came to the Avengers Campus, the word “appetizer” just made me think of fancy parties and chain restaurants, not everyday eats. (Seriously, the closest my dad ever came to serving an appetizer was making a plate of pizza rolls explode in the microwave.) But the innovative ideas coming out of the Pym Test Kitchen made me totally reconsider the concept of sharable snacks and starters. Their scientists took some of our favorite full-size foods and shrunk them into mouthwatering mini morsels, decreasing their dimensions without removing an ounce of flavor. Then they flipped the script, taking traditionally bite-size foods and enlarging them enough to feed an entire family. With nothing more than a quick quantum conversion, they offered up entirely new spins on classic favorites that grabbed attention and got everyone talking. And that’s exactly what an appetizer is supposed to do, isn’t it? Even better, the kitchen has been experimenting with more than just the size of the food—they’re exploring unique flavors from across the globe and beyond! From the familiar to the fantastical, the Pym Test Kitchen is always cooking up new signature snacks to be sampled and savored by everyone (no fancy party required).

YIELD: 1 SERVING

DIFFICULTY: EASY

QUANTUM PRETZEL
WITH CHEESE SAUCE

PREP TIME: 5 MIN > COOK TIME: 10 MIN

PRETZEL:

1 large pretzel, for serving (found in the freezer aisle of a grocery market)

CHEESE SAUCE:

2 tablespoons unsalted butter
2 tablespoons all-purpose flour
½ teaspoon onion powder
½ teaspoon garlic powder
½ teaspoon kosher salt
¼ teaspoon black pepper
⅛ teaspoon cayenne pepper
1 cup whole milk
8 ounces shredded cheddar cheese

Is there anything better than a warm, salty, soft pretzel? How about one that weighs a whopping 453.8 grams? A simple trip through the Pym Test Kitchen's ceiling-mounted Quantum Tunnel makes for a handheld treat so humongous that I can barely carry it back to the Worldwide Engineering BrigadeWorkshop on my own. Thankfully, my friends are always willing to help me transport it (and also eat it)! Luckily, what was once a single-serving snack works perfectly as a supremely sharable starter. In our lab, each pretzel is usually accompanied by a heated debate about which condiment is the perfect complement—cheese sauce or mustard. But no matter which side of the equation you're on (Team Cheese Sauce for the win!), I think we can all agree with this conclusion: The Quantum Pretzel is one of the Pym Test Kitchen's most successful (and popular) experiments for a very big reason! (No Pym Particles? No problem! Just use the biggest soft pretzel you can get your hands on! I promise it'll taste just as good!)

INSTRUCTIONS

1. In a large skillet over medium-low heat, melt the butter and whisk in the flour, onion powder, garlic powder, salt, pepper, and cayenne pepper. Cook until golden brown, 2 to 3 minutes.
2. Whisk in the milk and and cook for 5 to 7 minutes. Turn off the heat, then whisk in the cheese until smooth.
3. Serve with large pretzel.

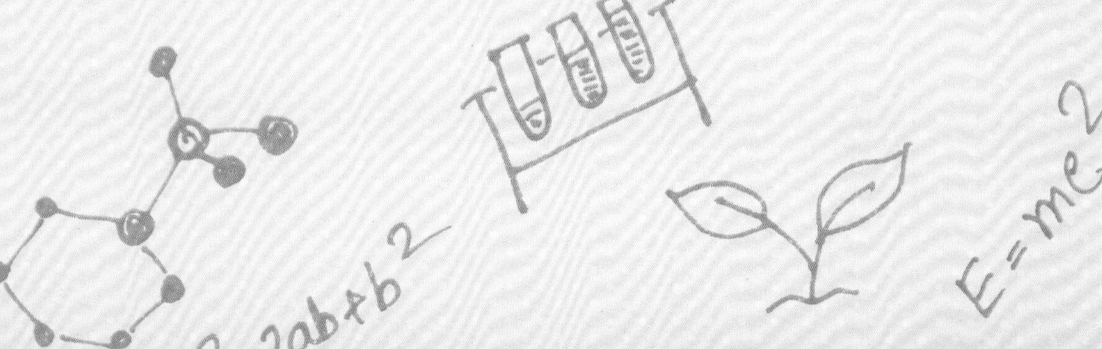

APPETIZERS

YIELD: 1 SERVING

DIFFICULTY: DIFFICULT

ATOMIC FUSION PRETZEL

PREP TIME: 20 MIN, PLUS AN ADDITIONAL 24 HOURS FOR PICKLING > COOK TIME: 25 MIN

Not all pretzels need to be "gigantified" (as my dad would say) to stand out from the crowd. Sometimes all it takes is a little creativity and some unexpected ingredients to put a new spin on something familiar. My dad came up with this "secret recipe" (which, let's be honest, isn't really all that secret anymore now that it's on the menu, but still), heaping Buffalo-style chicken on top of one of the Pym Test Kitchen's normal-size soft pretzels. The blazing heat from the sauce is balanced out by a perfect amount of coolness courtesy of celery, dill-pickled carrots, bleu cheese crumbles, and a ranch drizzle. Does this recipe technically qualify as science? I'm not sure, but the results are still undeniable. This one is too delicious to miss out on!

PICKLED CARROTS:

8 ounces white wine vinegar
2 ounces water
3 tablespoons granulated sugar
1 teaspoon minced fresh dill
1/2 teaspoon mustard seed
1/4 teaspoon kosher salt
1 garlic clove, peeled
1/2 bay leaf
3 carrots, quartered

BUFFALO CHICKEN:

1/4 cup buffalo hot sauce
1 tablespoon vegetable oil
1/4 teaspoon kosher salt
1/8 teaspoon black pepper
1 boneless skinless chicken thigh, diced

PRETZEL:

1 large pretzel, for serving
Buffalo chicken sauce (see below)
1 tablespoon ranch dressing
1 tablespoon bleu cheese crumbles
Pickled carrots (see below)
5 celery slices
3 celery leaves
1/4 teaspoon celery seed

INSTRUCTIONS

Make the pickled carrots:

1. In a large saucepan, combine the white wine vinegar, water, sugar, dill, mustard seed, salt, garlic, and bay leaf, and bring to a boil. Lower the heat and simmer for 10 minutes. Put the carrots in a bowl, then strain the hot brine through a sieve over the carrots. Cover and refrigerate overnight.

Make the Buffalo chicken:

2. In a medium bowl, stir together the hot sauce, oil, salt, and pepper until combined. Set aside 1 tablespoon for garnish. Add the chicken to the remaining sauce and toss to coat. Cover and refrigerate for 2 to 3 hours.
3. Preheat the oven to 375°F. Prep a baking sheet with parchment. Discard the marinade and place the chicken onto the prepped baking sheet. Bake to an internal temperature of 165°F, 20 minutes.

To add the pretzel and serve:

4. Warm the pretzel according to package directions. Place the pretzel onto a serving plate. Top with chicken, then drizzle the reserved Buffalo sauce and ranch dressing. Crumble the bleu cheese, then place the pickled carrots, celery, and celery leaves on top. Sprinkle the celery seed on top and serve.

YIELD: 16 SERVINGS

DIFFICULTY: MEDIUM

PYM PARTICLE PUPS

PREP TIME: 10 MIN > COOK TIME: 5 MIN

1-1¼ cups cake flour
1-1¼ cups yellow cornmeal
1 tablespoon baking powder
¼ teaspoon kosher salt
1 cup whole milk
¼ cup honey
1 large egg
1 quart vegetable oil, for frying
8 hot dogs, halved vertical
⅓ cup cornstarch

SPECIAL SUPPLIES:
16 wooden skewers
1 tall glass

When the Pym Test Kitchen first opened, they played with the idea of serving an enlarged corn dog that was approximately the size of my arm. It was insanely delicious, but totally impractical. See, the whole point of a corn dog is that you can carry it around easily while you eat it, which was definitely not the case here. In fact, the only ones who could manage to lift the thing were Thor (I guess that means he was worthy?) and Dr. Banner (because he's, you know, the Hulk). Since the whole point of the Pym Test Kitchen is to feed the world—not just two hungry, hungry heroes—they decided to revise the experiment's parameters and moved on to these micro-dogs instead for home chefs. I can confirm that they're equally tasty, but that hasn't stopped the Hulk from grumbling about them ever since.

INSTRUCTIONS >>>>>

1. In a medium bowl, whisk together the cake flour, cornmeal, baking powder, and salt.
2. Make a well in the center of the dry ingredients and stir in the milk, honey, and egg.
3. In a large saucepan over medium-high heat, heat the vegetable oil to 350°F.
4. Insert the skewers into the hot dogs, then roll in cornstarch. Pour batter into a tall glass and dip the hot dogs into the batter until coated.
5. Fry until browned, 2 to 3 minutes. Let drain on a wire rack.
6. Let cool slightly, then serve.

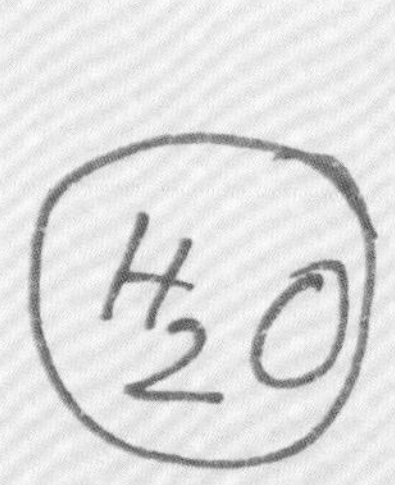

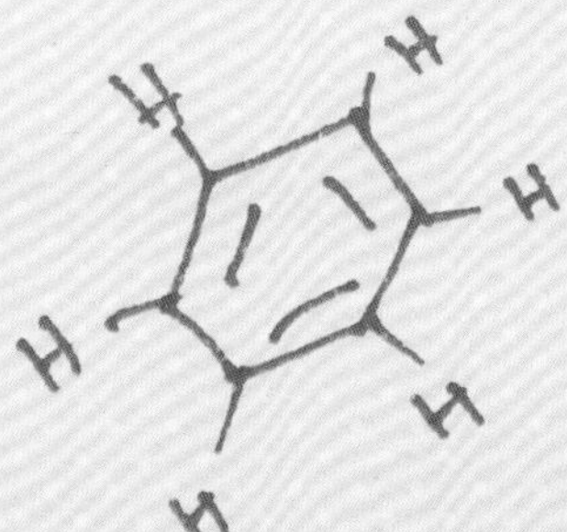

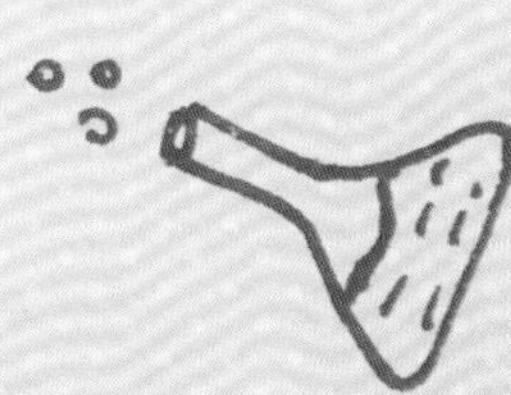

APPETIZERS

YIELD: 8 SERVINGS

DIFFICULTY: EASY

COSMIC KRACKLE CORN

PREP TIME: 15 MIN > COOK TIME: 5 MIN

8 cups popped salted popcorn
4 ounces red candy melts
4 ounces orange candy melts
2 ounces black candy melts
1 tablespoon silver round sprinkles

Sometimes the beauty of the unknown can inspire something unexpectedly delicious. Take this supercool candy-coated popcorn mix, for instance. It was something my dad came up with after getting trapped in the Quantum Realm—which is this weird subatomic dimension where time and space and science and magic all intersect. (Or at least that's what Dr. Pym says, and he's usually right about that kind of stuff.) Dad says that the skies in the Quantum Realm crackled and popped with colorful bursts of energy unlike anything he'd ever seen before. He said he couldn't quite do it justice in words, so he tried to recreate what he saw in food form, mixing colorful chocolate in with regular popcorn. He claims he still hasn't captured the look quite right . . . but when it comes to taste, I think he totally nailed it!

INSTRUCTIONS

1. Prep a baking sheet with parchment paper. Set aside.
2. In two separate microwave-safe bowls, melt the red and orange candy melts separately for 30 seconds, then two 15-second intervals. Stir until melted and smooth.
3. In a large bowl, lightly toss the popcorn with the orange and red melted candy coating. Spread the mixture onto the prepped baking sheet.
4. In a separate microwave-safe bowl, melt the black candy melts for 30 seconds, then two 15-second intervals. Stir until melted and smooth. Drizzle over the coated popcorn.
5. Sprinkle the silver sprinkles on top and let cool.
6. Once the candy melts have set, toss the popcorn and serve.

V GF

YIELD: 8 SERVINGS | DIFFICULTY: EASY

ANTS ON A LOG

PREP TIME: 10 MIN > COOK TIME: N/A

4 stalks celery
1/2 cup peanut butter
2 tablespoons dried fruit
2 tablespoons mini chocolate chips
2 tablespoons sunflower seeds
2 teaspoons chia seeds

Okay, okay, I know what you're thinking . . . "Ants on a log? That isn't science! It's a snack for babies!" Well, when your dad is Ant-Man, sometimes you've gotta lean into the theme a little, all right? And when we can take an old-school snack like this one and elevate it, maximizing its health benefits by adding protein-packed seeds and fresh fruits to the traditional celery and peanut butter base, it's clear why this reimagined classic shouldn't be limited to just kids anymore. But hey, if you're still too cool for it, that's totally fine. There'll just be more left over for me! (Pro tip: Don't be like my dad and name the "ants" on your log, okay? It makes eating them REALLY awkward.)

INSTRUCTIONS

1. Wash, dry, and trim the celery. Cut in half.
2. Spread the peanut butter over the celery. Sprinkle on the dried fruit, chocolate chips, sunflower seeds, and chia seeds to serve.

Yeah, I still feel pretty guilty about chomping down on "Ant May . . ."
–PETER

YIELD: 6 SERVINGS DIFFICULTY: MEDIUM

GOLDEN WAKANDA WEDGES

PREP TIME: 5 MIN > COOK TIME: 6 MIN

- 4 ripe plantains
- 4 tablespoons unsalted butter
- 1 teaspoon garlic salt
- ½ teaspoon cayenne pepper

Greetings, friends of Cassie Lang. I am Onome, member of the Worldwide Engineering Brigade and proud citizen of Wakanda. When Princess Shuri chose me to represent the best and brightest of our nation on the Avengers Campus, I could not decline such an opportunity. But since the state of California is a great distance from my home nation, I knew I would surely miss all that Wakanda has to offer. Thankfully, my peers at Worldwide Engineering Brigadesought to expand their horizons in more than just the field of science. They were eager to embrace the traditions and flavors of Wakanda—particularly these fried plantains, which have long been a staple of my people. And now that Cassie Lang has shown herself to be a true friend of Wakanda, I gladly share this recipe with her—and with you. May Bast bless your meal.

INSTRUCTIONS

1. Peel and slice the plantains into rounds.
2. Melt the butter in a large skillet over medium heat, then add the plantains. Cook for 3 minutes on each side until caramelized and browned. Let drain on a wire rack.
3. Sprinkle with garlic salt and cayenne pepper to serve.

V GF

YIELD: 12 SERVINGS | DIFFICULTY: MEDIUM

SUBATOMIC SLIDERS

PREP TIME: 20 MIN > COOK TIME: 30 MIN

When dad grew back to normal size after his time in the Quantum Realm, he said that the first thing he wanted to do was eat a hundred cheeseburgers. I told him that was physically impossible. I really should have known better—he immediately grew to giant-size and carried me to our local fast-food joint, where he found out that almost-Avengers don't eat for free. So, his all-beef dreams were put on hold until we came up with this recipe. One of his first acts was to convince their team to make a hundred burgers—"for science"—and shrink them down, all so he could complete a challenge I never actually set. (But to be fair, I managed to sneak one of these bite-size burgers, and I wouldn't mind eating a hundred of them myself.)

BURGERS:

2 pounds ground beef
1 tablespoon Worcestershire sauce
2 garlic cloves, minced
1 teaspoon basil
1 teaspoon onion powder
1/2 teaspoon black pepper
1/2 teaspoon kosher salt
3 slices Swiss cheese, quartered

TOPPING:

12 mini slider buns
1/2 cup sliced red onion
12 Roma tomato slices
1 cup arugula
12 gherkin pickles
Toothpicks

INSTRUCTIONS

1. Preheat the oven to 350°F. Prep a baking sheet with foil and place a wire rack on top of the foil.
2. In a large bowl, mix the ground beef, Worcestershire sauce, garlic, basil, onion powder, pepper, and salt until just combined. Divide into 12 equal balls and shape into patties.
3. Place patties onto the prepped baking sheet. Bake until juices run clear, 25 to 30 minutes. Top with Swiss cheese.
4. Place patty on a bottom slider bun. Top with onion, tomato, and arugula. Secure with a gherkin and a toothpick.

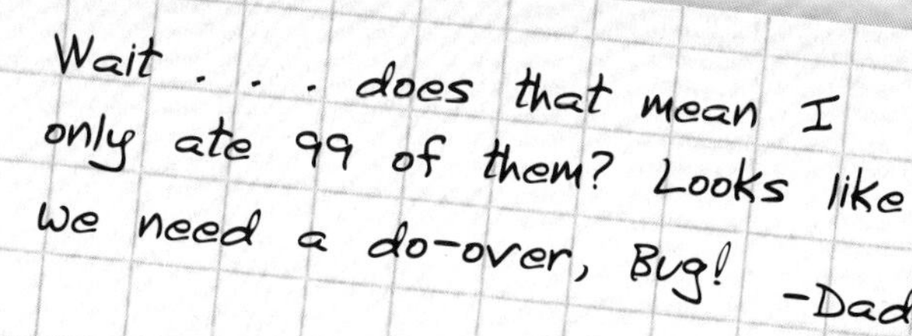
Wait . . . does that mean I
only ate 99 of them? Looks like
we need a do-over, Bug! -Dad

YIELD: 1 SERVING DIFFICULTY: EASY

SNACK MOLECULES

PREP TIME: 5 MIN > COOK TIME: N/A

2/3 cup popped popcorn
1/2 cup candied peanuts
1/2 cup sesame sticks
1/4 cup pretzels
1/4 cup popped sorghum

Craving that classic pretzel flavor but hoping for something a bit more portable (and maybe a touch less messy) than the other experimental versions on the menu? No worries! We've got you covered! At the end of each day, they shrink all of their extra-hot pretzels down to bite-size proportions. Then they take things to the next level by adding in honey-roasted peanuts and some amazing seasoned popped sorghum. The result is a snack mix that's the perfect blend of salty, sweet, and spicy. And when I say "perfect," I actually mean it: They ran all sorts of fancy scientific trials to determine the ideal flavor balance. One handful and I think you'll see why this combination was the clear winner!

INSTRUCTIONS

1. In a medium bowl, toss the popcorn, candied peanuts, sesame sticks, pretzels, and popped sorghum, and serve.

PYM
TEST KITCHEN
NAME
EXPERIMENT # 1710
RECIPE BY Scott L.
GEN. 20
TRIAL 9C
CAMPUS LAB

YIELD: 5 SERVINGS DIFFICULTY: MEDIUM

ACCUTECH R&D DUMPLINGS

PREP TIME: 30 MIN > COOK TIME: 10 MIN

Working at the Worldwide Engineering Brigade, we've had the opportunity to collaborate with a bunch of other divisions of Stark Industries, many of which have been extremely interested in supporting the scientific advancements being made by our team. It's always exciting to go on a field trip to see where the future is being forged, but on our visit to AccuTech R&D, we were all so focused on the sensational, spicy dumplings served during the welcome reception that we forgot to pay attention to the rest of the tour. Seriously, we spent, like, a solid three weeks trying to reverse engineer these little guys . . . and with some help from the experts at the Pym Test Kitchen, I think we finally got it right! Now, if we could only remember what AccuTech actually does . . .

SAUCE:

1/4 cup soy sauce
2 tablespoons Szechuan-style chili oil
1 tablespoon black vinegar
2 teaspoons light brown sugar
2 garlic cloves, minced
1 green onion, diced

DUMPLINGS:

8 ounces ground pork
2 garlic cloves, minced
2 tablespoons oyster sauce
1 tablespoon soy sauce
1 teaspoon fresh ginger, minced
1/4 teaspoon white pepper
25 wonton wrappers
1 green onion, diced

INSTRUCTIONS

Make the sauce:

1. In a small bowl whisk together the soy sauce, chili oil, black vinegar, brown sugar, garlic, and half the green onions. Set aside.

Make the dumplings:

2. In a medium bowl, mix together the ground pork, half the green onions (leaving a small amount in reserve), garlic, oyster sauce, soy sauce, ginger, and white pepper until just combined.
3. Place a teaspoonful of filling into the center of the wonton wrapper. Use your finger to add water onto two sides, folding up and creating a triangle shape. Pinch and fold the pointed corners downwards. Use water to tuck in the ends. Place onto a parchment-lined plate and cover with a towel. Repeat with the rest of the filling and wrappers.
4. Bring a large pot of water to a boil. Add the dumplings and gently stir to prevent them from sticking. Cook until they float to the surface, 2 minutes.
5. Strain the dumplings and place into a large bowl. To serve, pour the sauce over them and sprinkle with green onions.

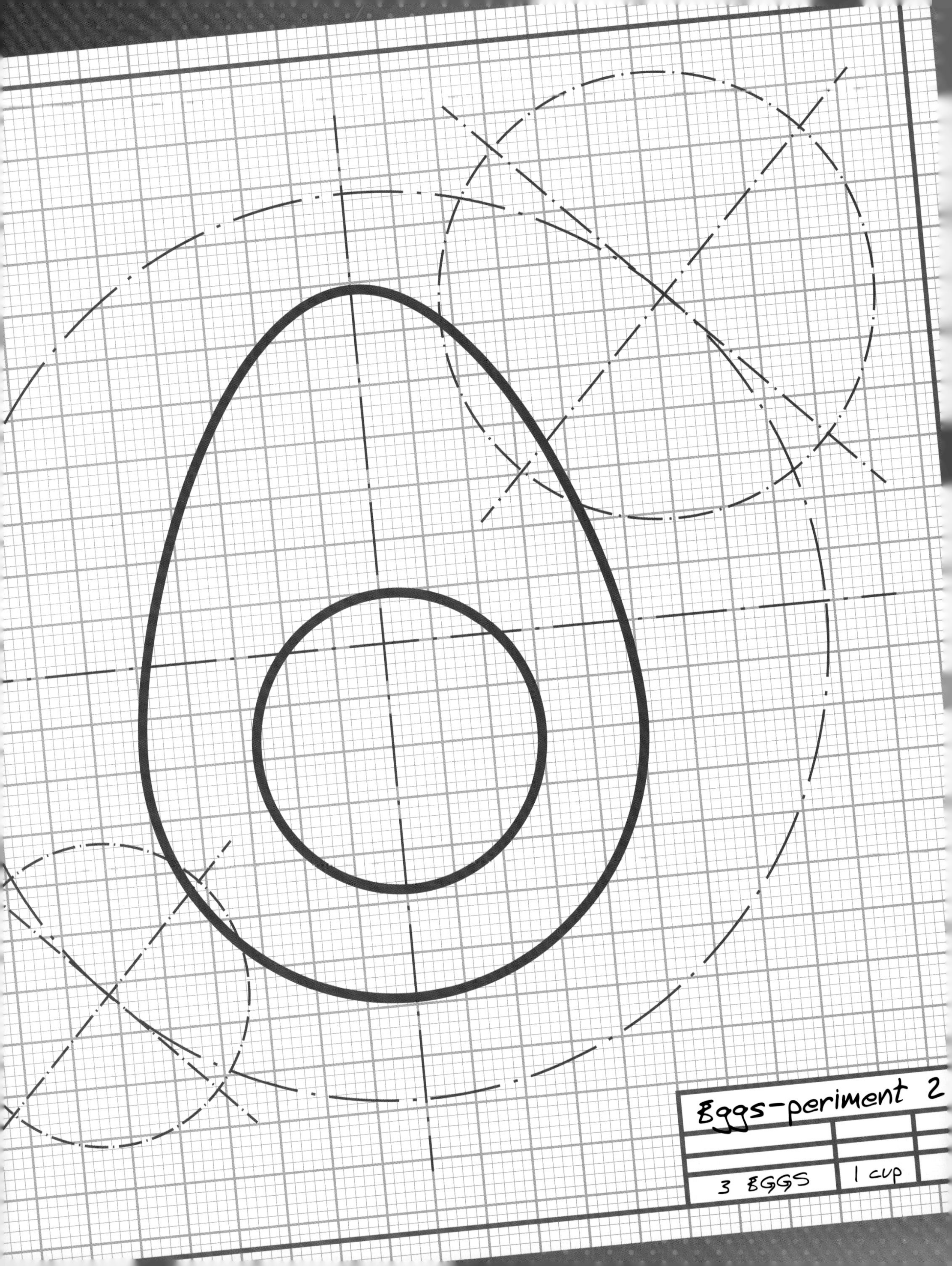
Eggs-periment 2
3 EGGS
1 cup

YIELD: 6 SERVINGS | DIFFICULTY: EASY

EGGS-PERIMENT 2.0

PREP TIME: 15 MIN > COOK TIME: 5 MIN

- 12 quail eggs
- Ice (for an ice bath)
- 2 tablespoons mayonnaise
- 1/2 teaspoon yellow mustard
- 1/8 teaspoon onion powder
- 1/8 teaspoon kosher salt
- 1/8 teaspoon white pepper
- 1/4 teaspoon paprika, for garnish

When it comes to who's in charge at the Pym Test Kitchen, the areas of expertise are pretty clear. Hope was selected to oversee everything related to sophisticated food science. Meanwhile, my dad put himself in charge of coming up with embarrassingly bad puns to identify all of the team's various experiments—or in this case, "eggs-periments." (I can't believe I actually just wrote that.) Believe it or not, these miniaturized deviled eggs aren't even the first item on the menu to bear this cringeworthy classification, but they certainly are the most unique. We got to sample a tray of these teeny-weeny eggs at a Pym Technologies fundraiser, and I can guarantee that they really are everything they're cracked up to be. (Oh no . . . I think he's rubbing off on me.)

INSTRUCTIONS

1. Place the quail eggs in a large saucepan. Fill with water, covering the eggs by about 1 inch. Bring to a boil. Turn off the heat and let stand for 2 to 3 minutes. Move eggs to an ice bath for 10 minutes, until cool.
2. Roll the eggs to crack and remove the shells. Carefully slice in half lengthwise, adding the yolks to a medium bowl and setting aside the whites.
3. In the bowl with the egg yolks, add the mayonnaise, mustard, onion powder, salt, and white pepper, stirring until just combined. Place in a piping bag and pipe into the egg whites. Sprinkle with paprika and serve.

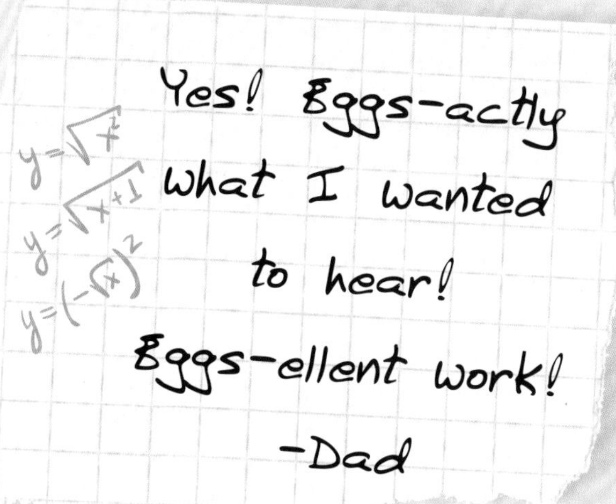

Yes! Eggs-actly
What I wanted
to hear!
Eggs-ellent work!
-Dad

V GF

YIELD: 3 SERVINGS DIFFICULTY: MEDIUM

RICE-OSCELES TRIANGLES

PREP TIME: 40 MIN > COOK TIME: 15 MIN

Appetizers may be fun to eat, but they've also earned the unfortunate reputation of being extremely unhealthy. Sure, they're full of flavor, but most of them have more calories than Hawkeye has arrows. So it's a good thing that the Pym Test Kitchen is always striving to push food beyond its preconceived boundaries. Just because something has been increased in size doesn't mean it should totally blow up your diet, right? The team managed to cover their bases (and most of the plate) with this starchy sensation—an enormous triangle of rice jam-packed with fresh veggies. As an extra added health bonus, this one happens to be both gluten-free and vegan! Sure, it's still a giant triangle of rice, so it's all comparative . . . but if you're in the mood for an app on the opposite end of the spectrum from smothered pretzels and corn dogs, this one covers all the angles!

RICE:

2 cups short grain rice
2½ cups water
3 tablespoons rice vinegar
2 tablespoons granulated sugar
½ teaspoon kosher salt

FILLING:

½ cup avocado, diced
¼ cup grated carrot
¼ cup cucumber, diced

GARNISH:

2 teaspoons furikake (rice seasoning)
½ large sheet nori (dried seaweed sheet)

INSTRUCTIONS

Make the rice:

1. Rinse the rice until water runs clear. Soak in cold water for 25 minutes, then drain.
2. In a large pot add the rice and water. Bring to a boil. Cover and reduce heat, then simmer for 15 minutes until the water is absorbed. Remove from heat and let sit for 10 minutes, covered.
3. Transfer the rice into a large bowl and fold in the rice vinegar, sugar, and salt. Let cool slightly.

Make the filling and garnish:

4. Scoop half of the rice onto a sheet of plastic wrap. Flatten and place the avocado, carrot, and cucumber in the center. Place the rest of the rice on top. Pull up the sides of the plastic to wrap the rice around the filling, forming a rice triangle shape. Sprinkle with furikake. Wrap rice ball with nori sheet to serve.

V V+ GF

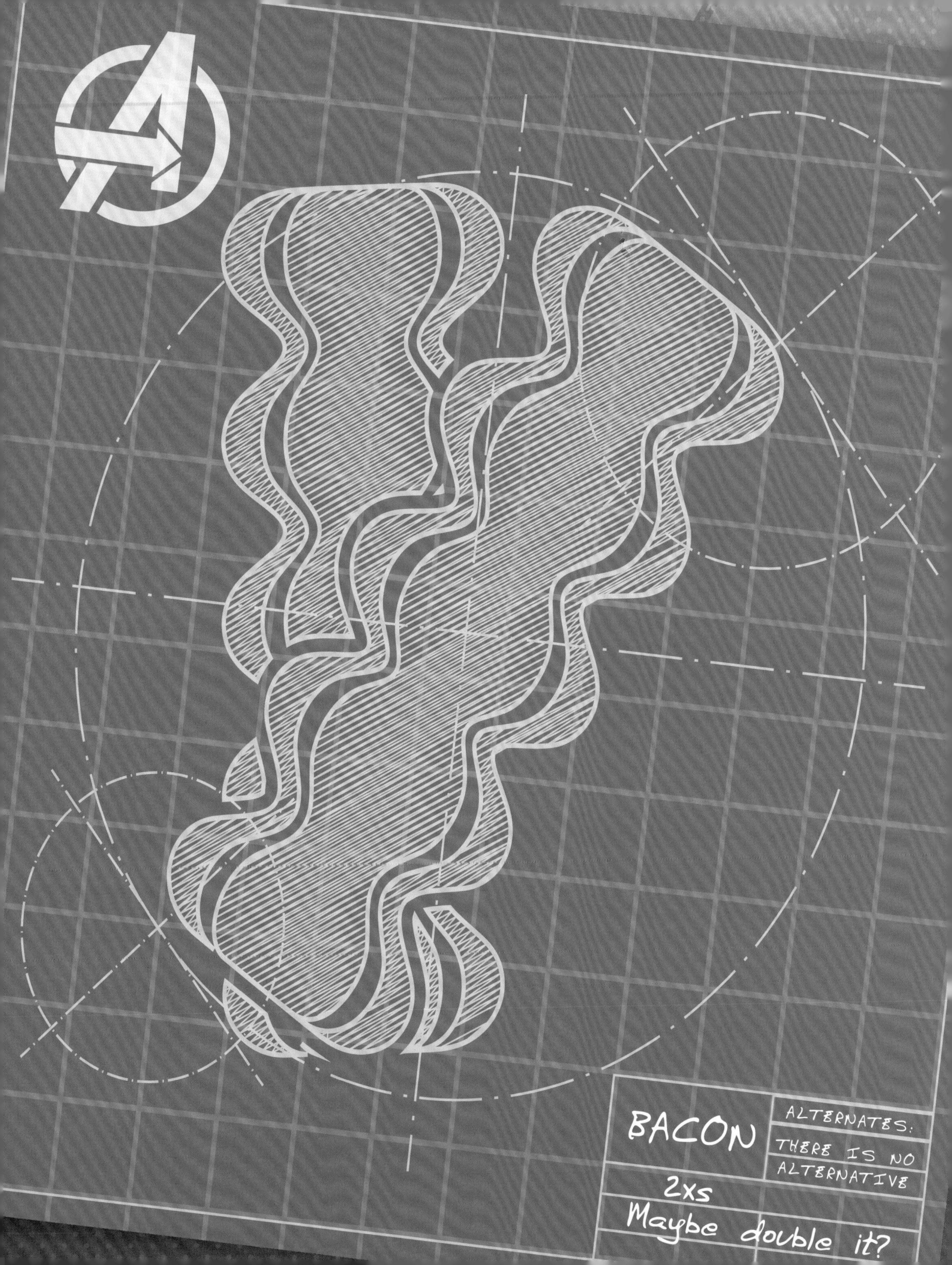
BACON
ALTERNATES:
THERE IS NO
ALTERNATIVE
2xs
Maybe double it?

YIELD: 8 SERVINGS　DIFFICULTY: EASY

BACON ANALYSIS

PREP TIME: 5 MIN > COOK TIME: 20 MIN

8 strips bacon
3 tablespoons maple syrup
1/3 cup finely chopped pecans (or sub with sunflower seeds)
1/4 teaspoon cayenne pepper

Of all the groundbreaking experiments that Pym Technologies has performed over the decades, this one may be the most important of them all. Sure, the Pym Test Kitchen is making my dreams of increased food supply and decreased waste a reality, but that's nothing compared to what they've achieved in the field of bacon. For so long, I falsely assumed that bacon was already the pinnacle of porcine perfection. But then they went and added this sweet, candied coating to it, making bacon even better—something I never fathomed was scientifically possible. The team hasn't made this recipe public yet, but I managed to sneak out their secret proprietary formula because the people deserve to know the truth! (I'm sure no one will mind. I mean, what's the worst that could happen?)

INSTRUCTIONS

1. Preheat the oven to 375°F. Prep a baking sheet by lining it with foil and placing a wire rack over the foil.
2. Lay down the bacon and evenly pour the maple syrup over it. Sprinkle with pecans and cayenne. Bake until browned, 17 to 20 minutes. Let cool for 2 to 3 minutes before serving.

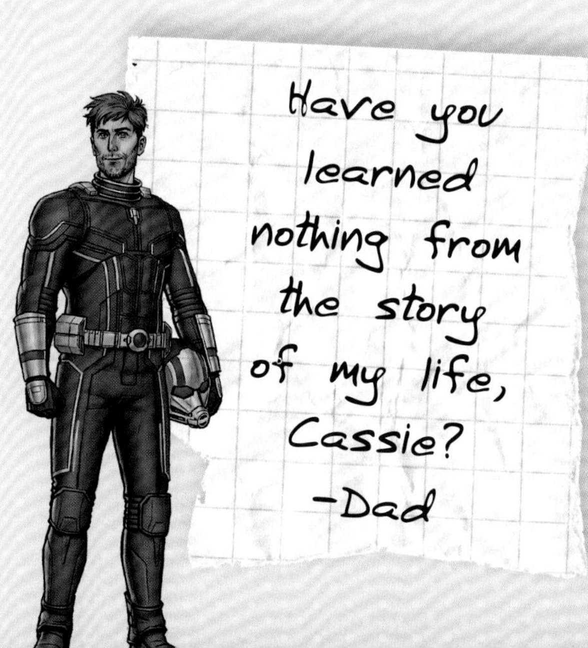

Have you learned nothing from the story of my life, Cassie?
-Dad

APPETIZERS

GF

CHAPTER 2

BIG BITES

MAIN DISHES

When I first stepped into the Pym Test Kitchen, I was totally blown away by what Dad and Hope had built together—a fully functioning state-of-the-art laboratory devoted entirely to scientific innovation through food, all based on my own original idea! I'll admit, it was a lot for a girl my age to digest—literally! When they brought out the first wave of edible experiments for me to try, I could hardly believe my eyes (or my stomach). From an enormous panini that could probably feed me for an entire week to a meatless meatball nearly the size of my head, it was clear that the scientists in the Test Kitchen weren't just breaking boundaries, they were having a blast doing it! Things that used to seem ordinary—like PB&J or grilled cheese—became extraordinary as the Pym team deconstructed and fine-tuned them to perfection. Of course, not every experiment was a smashing success (I'm looking at you, Oversized Olive Loaf), so we always made sure to have the number of our favorite pizza place on hand, just in case. But with way more hits than misses, the Pym Test Kitchen continues to push past culinary confines and serve up meals to astonish!

HAS A HEART

YIELD: 6 SERVINGS

DIFFICULTY: MEDIUM

PEPPER POTTS'S ARC REACTOR DISCS

PREP TIME: 20 MIN > COOK TIME: 30 MIN

When you're a teen like me, eating healthy isn't always the first thing on your mind. Sure, most days I try to make the best possible choices for my body and for the environment . . . but then other days, I can't resist scarfing down a Hulk-size burrito or a bucketful of mini corn dogs. Lucky for us, Stark Industries' own Pepper Potts does regular check-ins to make sure that all the kids at the Worldwide Engineering Brigade are taking proper care of themselves. And when she does, she usually brings us a wholesome, homemade lunch. One time, she served us these amazing vegetarian jackfruit tostadas. Her daughter Morgan helped her come up with the recipe, which plays off the shape of Tony Stark's original Arc Reactor (as a reminder of how heart-healthy the dish is). Thanks to Pepper, this nutritious meal has become an easy way to rescue any bad day!

JACKFRUIT:

Two 20-ounce cans young green jackfruit
1 tablespoon olive oil
1 chipotle in adobo, minced
4 garlic cloves, minced
1/3 cup orange juice
2 tablespoons fresh lime juice
2 teaspoons liquid smoke
2 teaspoons chili powder
2 teaspoons cumin
2 teaspoons oregano
1 teaspoon onion powder
1 teaspoon paprika
1 teaspoon kosher salt
1/2 teaspoon black pepper
1/4 cup salsa (any kind)

FOR SERVING:

8 corn tostadas
One 15-ounce can refried beans
1 cup guacamole
1 cup salsa
1 small red onion, sliced
1 small head iceberg lettuce, sliced
10 ounces queso fresco
1/2 cup crema
1/2 cup cilantro, chopped

INSTRUCTIONS

1. Drain and rinse the jackfruit, then squeeze out the water. Cut the jackfruit into smaller pieces and remove the core. Set aside.
2. In a skillet over medium-high heat, heat the olive oil and add the chipotle and garlic. Cook until softened, 2 to 3 minutes.
3. Add the jackfruit, orange juice, lime juice, liquid smoke, chili powder, cumin, oregano, onion powder, paprika, salt, and pepper. Cook until the jackfruit is softened, and the liquid has cooked down, 10 minutes. Toss with the salsa.
4. Preheat the oven to 400°F. Spread the jackfruit onto a parchment-lined baking sheet. Cook for 20 minutes.
5. To assemble, place a tostada on a plate. Spread with beans, then top with jackfruit. Spoon guacamole and salsa over the jackfruit. Add red onion and lettuce, then sprinkle with queso fresco (if desired). Drizzle crema and top with cilantro to serve.

V GF

OF ALL THE THINGS NAMED AFTER MY FATHER, THIS IS PROBABLY MY FAVORITE.

-HOPE

$$Ax + By + C = 0$$

$$\frac{x}{a} + \frac{y}{b} = 1$$

$$y - y_0 = k(x - x_0)$$

$$\frac{x - x_0}{x_1 - x_0} = \frac{y - y_0}{y_1 - y_0}$$

$$k = tg\varphi$$

$$x\cos\alpha + y\sin\alpha - p = 0$$

YIELD: 1 SERVING

DIFFICULTY: MEDIUM

PYM-INI

PREP TIME: 15 MIN > COOK TIME: 10 MIN

If you thought the Quantum Pretzel (page 15) was mind-blowingly massive, then just wait until you get your hands around a Pym-ini (if your hands are even big enough, which I doubt they are)! This supersized sammie is carefully constructed with salami, salame rosa, rosemary ham, provolone cheese, and sun-dried tomato spread, all placed with precision on a tasty, toasted focaccia. With a combo of flavors like that, it's a minor miracle that the Pym Test Kitchen doesn't run out of these babies the moment they open their doors. But that's where the science comes in! Sprinkle on a healthy dose of Pym Particles (which are totally safe for human consumption), and a single signature sandwich can be served in a multitude of magnitudes—from a "Teeny Pym-ini" for the kiddos to a huge table-size version that serves up to eight. Even though the size may vary, the flavors in this perfect panini always remain big and bold!

SAUCE:

- 2 tablespoons diced giardiniera vegetables
- 1 tablespoon diced sun-dried tomatoes
- 1/4 cup mayonnaise

SANDWICH:

- One 4-inch piece focaccia, sliced horizontally
- 2 slices hard salami
- 2 slices rosemary ham
- 2 slices rosa salami
- 1 slice provolone cheese
- 2 tablespoons unsalted butter

GARNISH:

- 1 small, sweet pepper
- 1 small pepperoncini pepper
- 1 dill gherkin pickle
- 1/4 cup marinara sauce, for serving

SPECIAL SUPPLIES:

- 1 small skewer

INSTRUCTIONS

1. With a small hand blender, blend the giardiniera vegetables and sun-dried tomatoes until smooth. Fold in the mayonnaise.
2. Spread the sauce on both sides of the focaccia. On the bottom piece, place the hard salami, then rosemary ham, rosa salami, and provolone cheese. Top with second piece of focaccia.
3. In a medium skillet over medium-high heat, melt the butter and add the sandwich. Place a heavy cast iron skillet on top, pressing down on the bread. Cook until golden brown, 4 minutes, then turn the sandwich over and repeat with the skillet press until the cheese has melted.
4. Place the sweet pepper, pepperoncini pepper, and pickle onto a small skewer, then poke it into the sandwich. Serve with marinara sauce.

YIELD: 4 SERVINGS

DIFFICULTY: EASY

PROPORTIONAL POULTRY POSTULATE

PREP TIME: 10 MIN, ADDITIONAL 8 HOURS FOR MARINATING > COOK TIME: 90 MIN

1/2 cup soy sauce
1/4 cup mirin
1/4 cup honey
2 garlic cloves, minced
One 2-inch slice fresh ginger
1/2 teaspoon Chinese five-spice powder
1/2 teaspoon kosher salt
1/2 teaspoon black pepper
4 turkey legs

Have you ever had the urge to swing around a huge hunk of meat like it is Mjølnir? Well, don't. I mean it. You'll only end up accidentally hitting one of your fellow young inventors in the head, resulting in what might be the world's first and only poultry-induced concussion the night before their big presentation at the Worldwide Engineering Brigade open house. (Or, you know, something equally traumatizing.) I guess what I'm trying to say here is that the experiments that come out of the Pym Test Kitchen may look wild and fun on the plate, but that's where they should stay. They are food first and serious science second . . . and at no point are they meant to be hurled about like an enchanted Asgardian weapon. (And I'm also trying to say that I'm really, really sorry about the turkey leg incident, Peter. Seriously.)

INSTRUCTIONS

1. In a medium bowl, whisk together the soy sauce, mirin, honey, garlic, ginger, Chinese five-spice, salt, and pepper. Pour into a sealable bag along with the turkey legs and marinate for 6 to 8 hours.
2. Preheat the oven to 375°F. Spray a wire rack with nonstick spray, and place onto a baking sheet lined with foil.
3. Remove the turkey legs and place onto the prepped pan, discarding the marinade.
4. Cook for 90 minutes or until an internal thermometer reads 165°F.

Forgiven! Just remind me to skip Thanksgiving at your place.
-Peter

YIELD: 1 SERVING

DIFFICULTY: EASY

PB3 SUPERB SANDWICH

PREP TIME: 15 MIN > COOK TIME: 20 MIN

CANDIED BACON:

2 slices bacon

1½ teaspoons packed light brown sugar

⅛ teaspoon kosher salt

SANDWICH:

2 slices white bread, toasted

2 tablespoons peanut butter

2 tablespoons strawberry jam

1 tablespoon crushed roasted peanuts

½ banana, sliced into planks

Who doesn't love a good old PB&J sandwich? I mean, seriously! Peanut butter and jelly are the perfect partners. They go together like Ant-Man and the Wasp! Like Cap and Bucky! Like Hawkeye and that new, cooler Hawkeye! It's a simple combo so flawless that altering the equation seems almost absurd . . . which made for a challenge that the flavor fanatics at the Pym Test Kitchen couldn't possibly resist! After exploring countless variations, they finally homed in on the "B" in "PB&J", taking the sandwich to new dimensions by adding in candied bacon and banana. It boosts the salty sweetness of a classic PB&J while adding in a savory component that pulls everything together in ways I never imagined possible. Served warm on Pym Particle–infused bread, this one is like comfort food cubed!

INSTRUCTIONS >>>>>>>

1. Preheat the oven to 375°F. Place the bacon on a baking sheet with parchment paper. In a small bowl, stir together the brown sugar and salt. Sprinkle the mixture evenly over the bacon. Bake for 17 to 20 minutes until the bacon is cooked and the sugar is caramelized. Set aside.
2. Spread peanut butter onto the toasted bread slices. Spread the jam on one side, then top with peanuts, bacon, and bananas. Place the second piece of bread on top, peanut butter side down, to sandwich. Cut on the diagonal to serve.

So much better than the PB-J3 with the jalapeños and jellybeans!
-Lunella

$V=a^3$

YIELD: 4 SERVINGS   DIFFICULTY: DIFFICULT

NOT SO LITTLE CHICKEN SANDWICH

PREP TIME: 1 HOUR > COOK TIME: 10 MIN

Why did the Worldwide Engineering Brigade kids cross the road? To go to the Pym Test Kitchen to eat this epic chicken sandwich, obviously! This crispy quantum-enlarged fried chicken breast bursts out of its brioche bun and is topped with tasty teriyaki, red chili sauce, and a crunchy pickled cabbage slaw. The size ratios might seem a little off to your eye, but I think you'll agree that the balance of flavors is spot-on exactly the way it is. (Plus, that little bun is soooo cute, right?) This sandwich instantly gained legendary status around the Avengers Campus, which kinda seems appropriate since Dad named it after an old storybook he always used to read me when I was a kid. Don't worry, though. The sky isn't falling . . . at least not today. (You never know around here.) But if it was, you could probably use this prodigious piece of poultry to shield yourself from any descending debris!

SLAW:
1 cup shredded green cabbage
1 cup shredded red cabbage
1 teaspoon minced green onions
1 tablespoon stemmed and minced cilantro
1/4 cup rice wine vinegar
2 tablespoons Dijon mustard
2 tablespoons teriyaki sauce
1 tablespoon orange juice
1 tablespoon vegetable oil
1 teaspoon sesame seeds
1/4 teaspoon kosher salt

TERIYAKI MAYONNAISE:
3 tablespoons mayonnaise
2 teaspoons teriyaki sauce
1/2 teaspoon rice wine vinegar

SRIRACHA MAYONNAISE:
3 tablespoons mayonnaise
1 teaspoon Sriracha
1/2 teaspoon rice wine vinegar

CHICKEN:
4 large boneless chicken breasts
1 cup all-purpose flour
1 teaspoon garlic powder
1 teaspoon onion powder
1 teaspoon paprika
1 teaspoon kosher salt
1 teaspoon black pepper
2 large eggs
1 1/2 cups panko breadcrumbs
1/2 teaspoon garlic powder
1/2 teaspoon onion powder
1/2 teaspoon paprika
1/2 teaspoon kosher salt
1/4 teaspoon black pepper
4 cups vegetable oil, for frying
4 brioche slider buns, toasted

INSTRUCTIONS

Make the slaw:

1. In a medium bowl, toss the green cabbage, red cabbage, green onions, and cilantro. Set aside.
2. In a small bowl, whisk the rice wine vinegar, Dijon mustard, teriyaki sauce, orange juice, vegetable oil, sesame seeds, and salt. Toss with the cabbage mixture. Cover and refrigerate.

Make the teriyaki mayonnaise:

3. In a small bowl, stir together the mayonnaise, teriyaki sauce, and rice wine vinegar. Cover and refrigerate.

Make the Sriracha mayonnaise:

4. In a separate small bowl, stir together the mayonnaise, Sriracha, and rice wine vinegar. Cover and refrigerate.

Make the chicken:

5. Pound out and flatten the chicken breast between two pieces of plastic wrap until it's 1/4-inch thick. Set aside.
6. Create a dredging station: In the first bowl, whisk the flour, garlic powder, onion powder, paprika, salt, and pepper. Crack the eggs into the second bowl and lightly beat. In the third bowl, stir together the panko, garlic powder, onion powder, paprika, salt, and pepper.
7. Add oil to a large skillet over medium heat and heat to 350°F. Dredge the chicken in the flour, shaking off the excess, then do the same with the egg and then the panko mixture. Fry 3 to 4 minutes on each side until golden brown and at an internal temperature of 165°F.
8. Place the bottom of the slider bun onto a serving plate. Add the chicken, then drizzle on the teriyaki mayonnaise, then the Sriracha mayonnaise. Place the slaw on top, then add the top bun to serve.

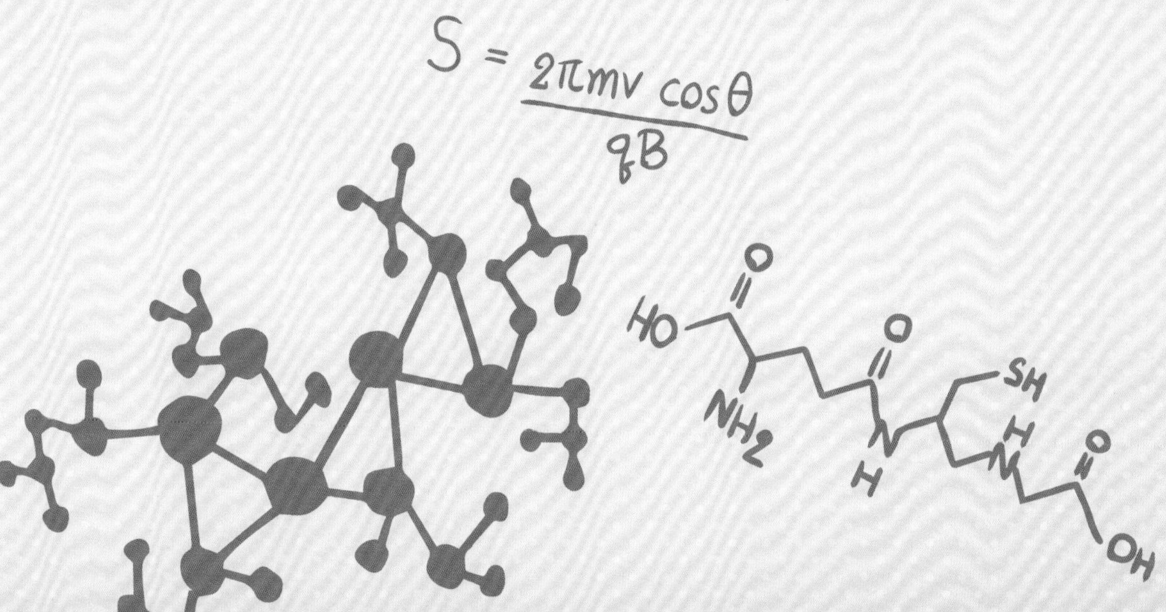

PYM
© Disney © MARVEL

YIELD: 8 SERVINGS DIFFICULTY: EASY

LUCKY DOG'S PIZZA

PREP TIME: 15 MIN > COOK TIME: 15 MIN

- 1 tablespoon cornmeal
- Pre-made pizza dough
- $\frac{1}{2}$ cup pizza sauce
- $2\frac{1}{2}$ cups shredded mozzarella cheese
- 1 cup sliced ham
- 4 to 5 slices bacon, cooked and chopped
- $\frac{1}{2}$ cup sliced pepperoncini peppers
- $\frac{1}{3}$ cup peanut butter

I vote bacon!
-Peter

Ham!
-Lunella

When we really get in the groove on a project, the Worldwide Engineering Brigade team tends to put in some pretty late hours in the lab. Once the Pym Test Kitchen closes its doors and the Shawarma Palace cart rolls away for the evening, there aren't many options left to calm the inevitable late-night grumbling of our teenage tummies. So when we start to get those after-hour urges, we know it's time to get Lucky! And by that, I mean it's time to get pizza from our favorite local delivery joint, Lucky Dog's! Of course, with all the unique perspectives we have on our team, it always makes the decision about what toppings to get nearly impossible . . . so we usually end up getting them all! I'm not sure this creative combo would pass the test at the Pym Test Kitchen, but it sure keeps us pretty happy! "Who's a good pizza?" (You are!)

INSTRUCTIONS

1. Preheat the oven to 475°F. Spray a pizza pan with nonstick spray and sprinkle the cornmeal on top. Roll out the dough onto the pan.
2. Evenly spread the pizza sauce on top, then sprinkle the mozzarella. Add the ham, bacon, and pepperoncini. Bake in the oven until the cheese has melted, 10 to 12 minutes.
3. Place the peanut butter in a microwave-safe bowl and cook for 15 seconds. Stir and cook for another 15 seconds, just until pourable. Drizzle onto the pizza. Serve immediately.

PEANUT BUTTER!
-DOREEN

$a^2 = b^2 + c^2 - 2bc \cos A$

Potatoes? No?
Maybe next time...
-Harley

HOT PEPPERS!
-ONOME

YIELD: 1 SERVING

DIFFICULTY: DIFFICULT

IMPOSSIBLE™ SPOONFUL

PREP TIME: 20 MIN > COOK TIME: 1 HOUR

The food scientists at the Pym Test Kitchen are determined to take impossible ideas and make them possible. One of those ideas involves drastically reducing our impact on the environment by exploring meatless options that taste just as good as—or even better than—their traditional counterparts. This pasta dish might not seem all that out of the ordinary (other than the fact that it gets served in a supersize spoon), but there's a secret you might not notice at first glance—or even at first bite! When it comes to the mix of mini and massive meatballs, the "meat" part is actually 100% plant-based. No, really! Even the cheese is dairy-free! (How cool is that?) I totally get that some people are still hesitant to go meatless, but if plant-based options can taste as good as this, I have a feeling they'll eventually change their minds. After all, this dish is proof that anything is possible!

MEATBALL:

2/3 cup extra-firm tofu
1 garlic clove
2 tablespoons minced white onion
1 tablespoon vegetable oil
1/4 cup minced button mushrooms
1/4 cup minced cremini mushrooms
1/4 cup minced shiitake mushrooms, stems removed
1 tablespoon minced shallot
2 garlic cloves, minced
1/4 teaspoon kosher salt
12 ounces Impossible™ burger
1/2 cup dairy-free Parmesan cheese
2 tablespoons panko breadcrumbs
2 teaspoons chopped fresh Italian parsley leaves
1/2 teaspoon Italian seasoning

FOR SERVING:

1/2 cup rigatoni
1/2 cup ditalini
1/2 cup marinara sauce, warmed
1 1/2 teaspoons dairy-free Parmesan cheese
3 to 4 sprigs micro basil, for garnish

V

V+

RECIPE CONTINUES ON NEXT PAGE...

INSTRUCTIONS

Make the meatball:

1. In the base of a blender, add the extra-firm tofu, garlic clove, and onion. Blend until smooth. Set aside.
2. Heat the vegetable oil in a medium skillet over medium heat and add the button mushrooms, cremini mushrooms, shiitake mushrooms, shallot, and minced garlic. Cook until the mushrooms have cooked down, 7 to 10 minutes. Season with salt and let cool.
3. In a large bowl, mix together the Impossible™ meat, Parmesan cheese, panko breadcrumbs, Italian parsley, Italian seasoning, the tofu garlic spread (see step 1), and the cooled mushroom mixture. Form into one meatball.
4. Preheat to 375°F. Prep a baking pan with parchment. Bake to an internal temperature of 160°F, 40 minutes, until even browned.

For serving:

5. Fill 3/4 of a large saucepan with water and bring to a boil. Cook pasta for 10 to 12 minutes. Drain but do not rinse. Toss with marinara sauce and pour into a serving dish. To serve, top with Impossible meatball, Parmesan cheese, and micro basil.

FROM THE DESK OF

HOPE VAN DYNE, DIRECTOR

After a multi-year hiatus, Pym Technologies is proud to join the Avengers Campus to re-establish our operations and share our revolutionary "Pym Particles" technology with the public.

When my father, Dr. Hank Pym, first discovered Pym Particles—particles that can shrink any object to the size of an insect or grow it to gigantic scale—he created suits so that the heroes known as Ant-Man and The Wasp could use Pym Particles to become the perfect size for any mission. But that was just the beginning...

From sustainable shipping and recycling programs to innovations in food sciences and miniaturized farming, Pym Technologies is on a mission to find new ways of using Pym Particles to help the world.

SHRINKING PROBLEMS. GROWING SOLUTIONS.

YIELD: 4 SERVINGS

DIFFICULTY: MEDIUM

NEW YORK'S TASTIEST SHAWARMA

PREP TIME: 10 MIN, ADDITIONAL 24 HOURS FOR MARINATING > COOK TIME: 20 MIN

MARINADE:

3/4 cup lemon juice
1/3 cup vegetable oil
5 garlic cloves, minced
1 teaspoon kosher salt
1 teaspoon ground cardamom
1 teaspoon ground coriander
1 teaspoon ground cumin
1 teaspoon smoked paprika
1/2 teaspoon black pepper
1/2 teaspoon cayenne pepper
1 pound diced boneless, skinless chicken thighs

GARLIC SAUCE:

1/2 cup vegetable oil, divided in half
1/4 cup water
2 teaspoons lemon juice
6 garlic cloves
1/4 teaspoon kosher salt

SHAWARMA:

4 pieces naan bread

The Pym Test Kitchen is amazing, but it's not the only place to eat on the Avengers Campus. When we're in a hurry—or we're just not in the mood to be gastronomical guinea pigs—we hit the Shawarma Palace food cart right across from the Worldwide Engineering Brigade Workshop (near the Ancient Sanctum). The cart is run by Jimmy, one of the Avengers' biggest fans, whose original NYC restaurant gained a lot of unexpected attention when Earth's Mightiest Heroes grabbed a victory meal there after the Battle of New York. When the Avengers Campus opened, the owner brought his now-famous shawarma to the west coast—and we're totally thrilled that he did! These mouthwatering wraps might not be scientifically scrutinized like every dish served at the Pym Test Kitchen, but sometimes the best recipes don't come from the lab—they come from the heart.

SHAWARMA PALACE

EST. 1963

$i_C = I_m \sin(\omega t$

$F = qvB$

$P_m = \frac{I_m V_m}{2}$

$F = \frac{kQ_1Q_2}{r^2}$

$E = mc^2$

RECIPE CONTINUES ON NEXT PAGE...

INSTRUCTIONS

Make the marinade:

1. In a small bowl, whisk the lemon juice, vegetable oil, garlic, salt, cardamom, coriander, cumin, paprika, black pepper, and cayenne pepper. Pour into a sealable bag along with the chicken and toss to coat. Refrigerate overnight.

Make the garlic sauce:

2. In the base of a small blender, combine 1/4 cup vegetable oil, water, lemon juice, garlic, and salt. As it blends, pour in a steady stream of the remaining oil until emulsified. Cover and refrigerate the garlic sauce until ready to use.

Make the shawarma:

3. Preheat oven to 375°F. Place the chicken onto a foil lined baking sheet, discarding the marinade. Bake until cooked through to an internal temperature of 165°F, 20 minutes.
4. Place the naan bread onto a large piece of foil. Spread garlic sauce onto the naan. Top with 1/4 of the chicken, then roll tight, wrapping in the foil. Repeat with the remaining naan and chicken, then serve.

You are always my favorite, Cassie!
7% discount for you every second Tuesday!
-Jimmy

SHAWARMA PALACE
SHAWARMA FLAVORS FOR HEROES ON THE GO!
SHAWARMA
SHAWARMA
SMASH

YIELD: 4 SERVINGS DIFFICULTY: DIFFICULT

IMPOSSIBLE™ VICTORY FALAFEL SHAWARMA

PREP TIME: 30 MIN > COOK TIME: 20 MIN

While the Shawarma Palace's chicken wrap might be the most popular item on their menu, they proudly offer other "Shawarma Flavors for Heroes on the Go!" One of those alternate options swaps out seasoned chicken for crispy, plant-based falafel, cauliflower, and a creamy hummus. With that simple change, this version goes completely vegan. The rest of the wrap's beloved ingredients—including the garlic spread and pickled veg—all stay exactly the same. I mean, if it already works, why change it? (I read that on a poster in the Worldwide Engineering Brigade break room.) The similarities between both wraps will make recreating the magic at home a bit easier, too, since I can make big batches of condiments, then swap out the fillings depending on my mood (which, according to Mom, changes more often than Dad's size). Whether you're going with chicken or falafel, this shawarma is definitely a win-win!

GARLIC SAUCE:

1/2 cup vegetable oil, divided in half
1/4 cup water
2 teaspoons lemon juice
6 garlic cloves
1/4 teaspoon kosher salt

SPICED CAULIFLOWER:

1 cup cauliflower florets
1 tablespoon olive oil
1/2 teaspoon ground cumin
1/2 teaspoon paprika
1/4 teaspoon black pepper
1/4 teaspoon cayenne pepper

FALAFEL:

3/4 cups falafel mix
1/2 cups water
3/4 cups Impossible™ burger
1 tablespoon diced red onion
1 tablespoon minced Kalamata olives
2 teaspoons minced fresh mint
1/2 teaspoon ground cardamom
1/2 teaspoon ground coriander
1/2 teaspoon ground cumin
1/2 teaspoon paprika
1/4 teaspoon kosher salt
1/4 teaspoon black pepper
1/4 teaspoon cayenne pepper
1/4 teaspoon ground sumac
1/4 teaspoon cinnamon
2 cups vegetable oil, for frying

SHAWARMA:

4 pieces pita bread, warmed
1/2 cup hummus

V V+

INSTRUCTIONS

Make the garlic sauce:

1. In the base of a small blender, add 1/4 cup vegetable oil, water, lemon juice, garlic, and salt. As it blends, pour in a steady stream of the remaining oil until emulsified. Cover and refrigerate the garlic sauce until ready to use.

Make the cauliflower:

2. Preheat oven to 450°F. In a large bowl, toss the cauliflower, olive oil, cumin, paprika, black pepper, and cayenne pepper. Spread out onto a baking sheet. Roast for 15 to 17 minutes until crispy and lightly charred.

Make the falafel:

3. In a medium bowl, mix together the falafel mix and water. Set aside.
4. In a large bowl, mix together the Impossible™ burger, red onion, Kalamata olives, mint, cardamom, coriander, cumin, paprika, salt, black pepper, cayenne, pepper, sumac, and cinnamon. Add the falafel mix and combine. Form 12 balls.
5. Add oil to a large skillet over medium heat and heat to 350°F. Fry falafel until golden brown and at an internal temperature of 135°F, 3 to 4 minutes.

Make the shawarma:

6. Place the pita bread onto a large piece of foil. Spread the garlic sauce onto the pita, then the hummus. Top with the falafel and the cauliflower. Roll tight, wrapping in the foil, to serve.

SHAWARMA
PALACE
SHAWARMA FLAVORS FOR HEROES ON THE GO!
SUPER FOOD
SUPER SERVICE
NYC'S BEST
NOW AVAILABLE ON

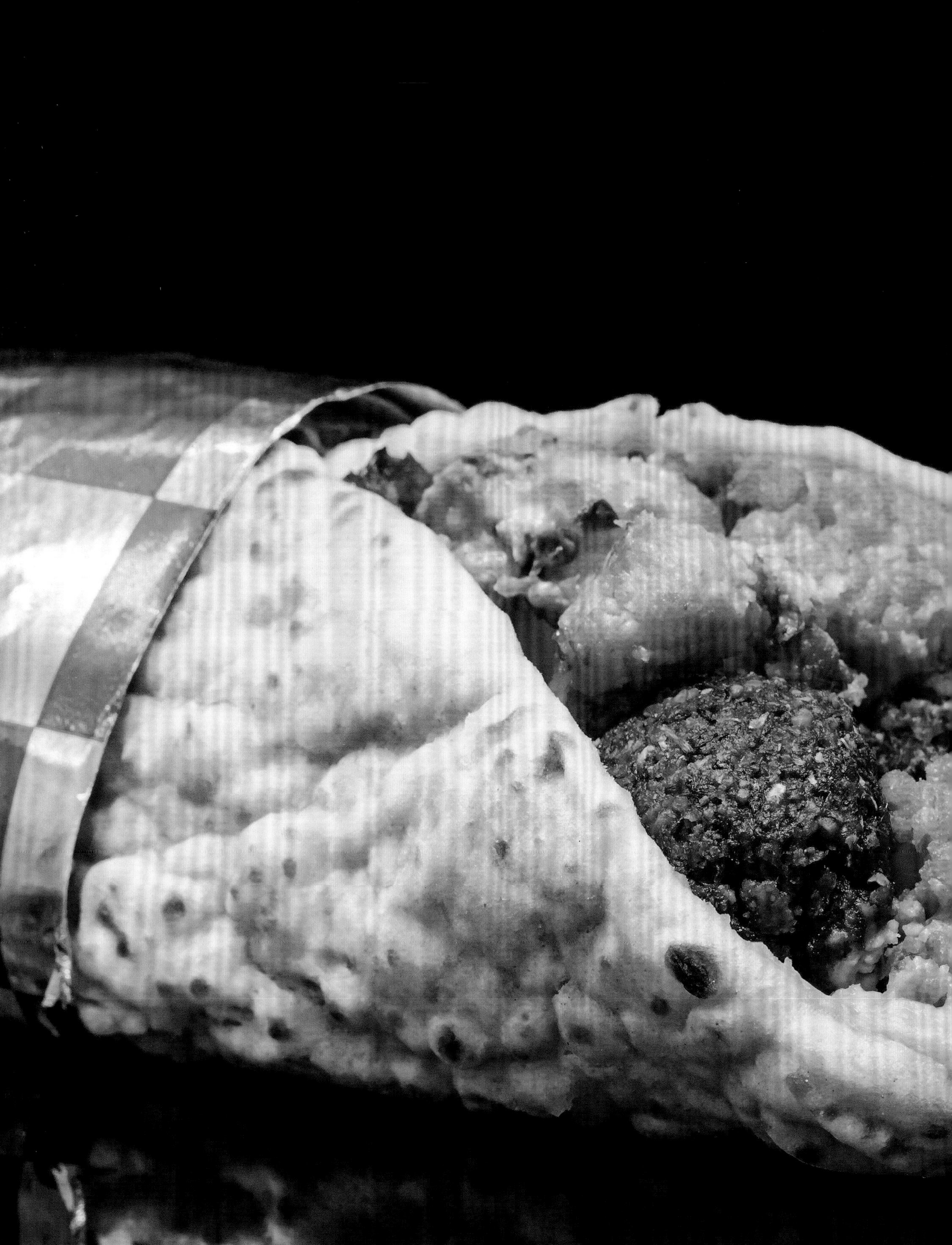

YIELD: 4 SERVINGS

DIFFICULTY: DIFFICULT

GAMMA BURRITO

PREP TIME: 15 MIN > COOK TIME: 30 MIN

Despite what the name of this dish suggests, Hope wanted me to make it unconditionally clear that "the Pym Test Kitchen does not use rays—or any other form of potentially harmful radiation—in the preparation of any of its food-based experiments." Okay, now that we've got the disclaimer off our plate, let's focus on what's actually still on it: one behemoth of a burrito! Coming from the Bay Area, I grew up with good burritos around every corner, but you're not going to find anything like this in the Mission District. This Cal-Mex colossus instantly stands out because of its scaled-up size and its gamma-green tortilla, but it's the fresh fillings packed inside that make this monster truly incredible. The Hulk can eat 17.5 of these bad boys (we counted), but if you manage to polish off just one of them, I think you earn official hero status!

RICE:

1 tablespoon olive oil
1/4 cup chopped onion
1 garlic clove, minced
1/2 cup uncooked white rice
3/4 cup chicken broth
1/2 cup diced tomatoes
2 tablespoons diced green chiles
1 teaspoon chili powder
1/2 teaspoon cumin
1/2 teaspoon oregano
1/2 teaspoon paprika
1/2 teaspoon kosher salt
1/2 teaspoon black pepper

MEAT:

3/4 pound ground beef
1 tablespoon chili powder
1 teaspoon cumin
1/2 teaspoon garlic powder
1/2 teaspoon onion powder
1/2 teaspoon paprika
1/4 teaspoon kosher salt
1/4 teaspoon black pepper

BURRITO:

Six 8-inch spinach tortillas
14 ounces refried beans, warmed
1 cup shredded cheddar cheese
1/3 cup guacamole
1/3 cup salsa
2 tablespoons crema
2 teaspoons hot sauce

RECIPE CONTINUES ON NEXT PAGE...

INSTRUCTIONS >>>>>

Make the rice:

1. In a medium skillet over medium heat, add the olive oil. Add the onion and garlic and cook until soft, about 3 to 4 minutes. Stir in the rice and cook until lightly toasted, 2 to 3 minutes.
2. Stir in the chicken broth, tomatoes, green chiles, chili powder, cumin, oregano, paprika, salt, and pepper. Bring to a boil, then reduce heat to low and cover. Simmer until the liquid has been cooked down, 20 minutes. Fluff rice and set aside. Cover to keep warm.

Make the meat:

3. In a separate medium skillet over medium heat, cook the ground beef until browned, 5 to 7 minutes. Stir in the chili powder, cumin, garlic powder, onion powder, paprika, salt, and pepper. Cook 2 to 3 minutes more, until fragrant.

Make the burritos:

4. Lay out the 6 tortillas on a large sheet of aluminum foil, overlapping the edges. Spread out the refried beans, then top with cheese. Spread out the rice, then add the ground beef. Top with guacamole, salsa, crema, and hot sauce.
5. Tuck in the edges and carefully roll into a giant burrito. Slice to serve.

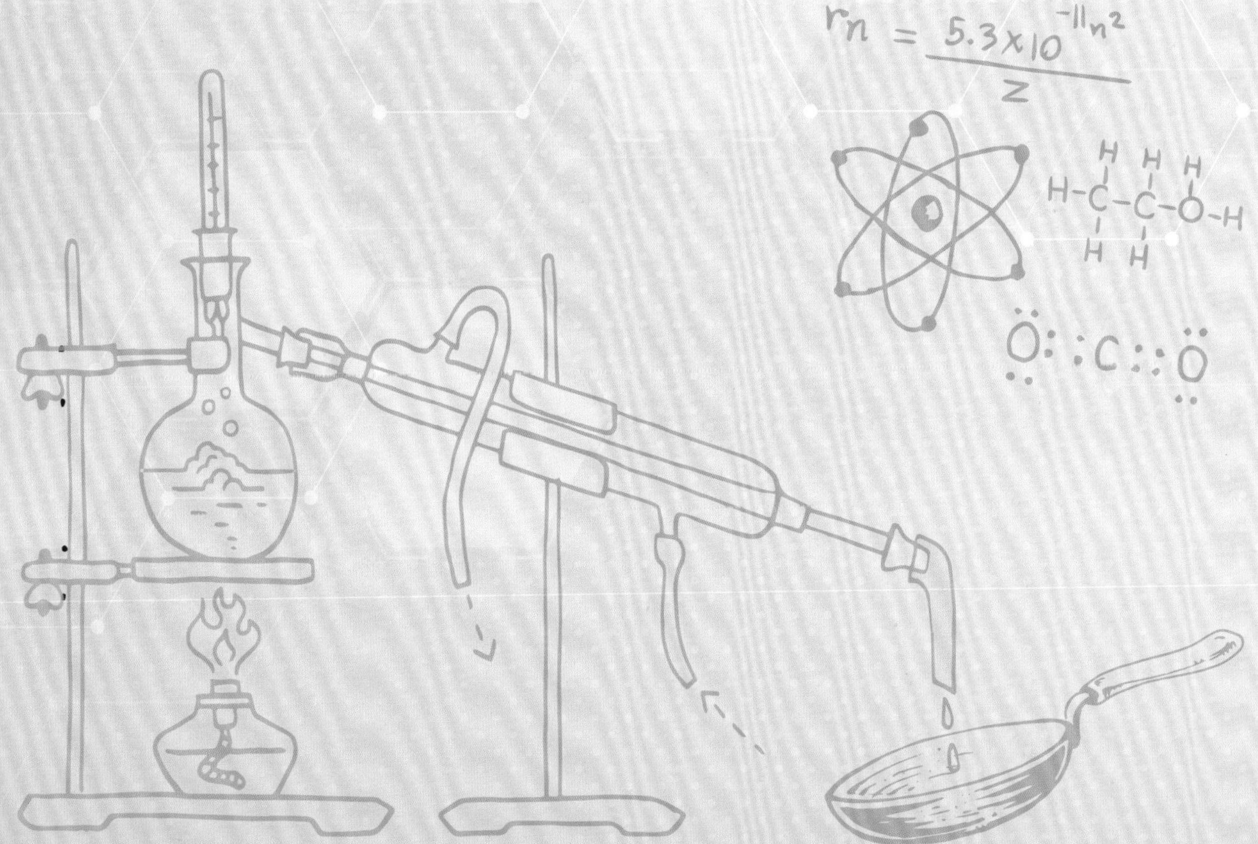

YIELD: 8 SERVINGS   DIFFICULTY: MEDIUM

SOUP AND SANDWICH SYMMETRY

PREP TIME: 30 MIN > COOK TIME: 45 MIN

Sometimes, science is about pushing existing configurations beyond accepted parameters. But other times, it's about taking what already exists and refining it down to its ultimate form. When it comes to grilled cheese and tomato soup, there's really not a whole lot of improvement needed. Sure, I guess you could level both elements up in shocking and exciting new ways, but there's also something to be said for the beauty of simplicity. So instead of going the same route they did with the PB3 Superb Sandwich (page 45), the Pym Test Kitchen team veered hard in the opposite direction here, paring things down and playing with sizes and ratios to achieve a seamless state of soup and sandwich stasis. That might not sound like a lot of fun on the surface, but once you get to float the grilled cheeses in your soup like croutons to soak up all that tomatoey goodness, it all makes perfect sense.

SOUP:

2 tablespoons olive oil
1 large onion, diced
1 carrot, diced
4 garlic cloves, minced
1 tablespoon tomato paste
12 ounces vegetable stock
Two 14-ounce cans diced tomatoes
2 tablespoons light brown sugar
1 tablespoon basil
1 tablespoon oregano
2 teaspoons kosher salt
1 teaspoon paprika
1 teaspoon black pepper
½ cup coconut milk
⅓ cup basil leaves

GRILLED CHEESE:

4 slices white bread
4 tablespoons unsalted butter, softened
4 slices Cheddar cheese
4 slices Swiss cheese

INSTRUCTIONS

Make the soup:

1. In a Dutch oven over medium heat, add the olive oil, onion, and carrot. Cook until softened, 5 minutes.
2. Add the garlic and cook until fragrant, 1 minute. Stir in the tomato paste and cook for 1 minute more.
3. Pour in the vegetable stock, tomatoes, brown sugar, basil, oregano, salt, paprika, and pepper. Bring to a boil, then reduce heat to low. Simmer for 45 minutes.
4. Turn off the heat and stir in the coconut milk. Use an immersion blender to puree until smooth.

Make the grilled cheese:

5. Spread 1 tablespoon butter onto one side of each slice of bread. Place two slices, buttered side down, into a skillet over medium heat. Add the cheese, then top with the remaining two slices of bread (buttered side up). Cook for 2 minutes on each side until the bread has browned and the cheese has melted. Cut the sandwiches into quarters.
6. Ladle soup into bowls and top with fresh basil to serve.

YIELD: 6 SERVINGS

DIFFICULTY: MEDIUM

WANDA'S SOKOVIAN PAPRIKASH

PREP TIME: 30 MIN > COOK TIME: 1 HOUR

As you can imagine, we get our fair share of visitors at the Worldwide Engineering Brigade Workshop, from tourists to tech moguls—and even the occasional villain bent on world domination! But there's still nothing more exciting than the days when an actual Avenger comes to our corner of campus. (Yeah, I know my dad is a certified super hero, but he doesn't count.) They may be Earth's Mightiest Heroes, but they never make us feel like we're less important than they are, even though we're just kids. Sometimes they even invite us over to Avengers Headquarters for dinner! I recommend going on Sundays. Wanda Maximoff makes a traditional paprikash that is absolutely unreal! There's something magical about it that instantly lifts your spirits. She even gave me the recipe, along with an important reminder to always double-check the spices. Apparently, it's not a proper paprikash if it doesn't have paprika—so this one doubles down with two kinds: sweet and hot (kinda like Wanda herself)!

CHICKEN:

- 2 pounds chicken thighs
- 1 teaspoon kosher salt
- 1/2 teaspoon black pepper
- 2 tablespoons unsalted butter
- 1 tablespoon olive oil
- 1 large onion, sliced
- 3 garlic cloves, minced
- 2 1/2 tablespoons sweet paprika
- 1 teaspoon hot paprika
- 14 ounces chicken broth
- 2 tablespoons cornstarch
- 1/2 cup sour cream

NOODLES:

- 12 ounces egg noodles, for serving
- 1 tablespoon unsalted butter
- 1 tablespoon chopped parsley, for serving

INSTRUCTIONS

Make the chicken:

1. Season the chicken with salt and pepper. Set aside.
2. In a Dutch oven over medium-high heat, add the butter and olive oil and cook the chicken until browned, 4 to 5 minutes on each side. Remove to a plate and set aside.
3. Add the onion and garlic and cook until soft, 2 to 3 minutes. Turn heat to low and stir in the sweet paprika and hot paprika.
4. Whisk in the chicken broth, then add the chicken back to the pot, nestling into the liquid. Cover and cook for 45 minutes.

Make the noodles, and serve:

5. Bring a large pot of water to a boil and cook the noodles according to package directions. Drain but do not rinse. Toss with butter and place on a serving plate. Remove the chicken and place on top of the noodles.
6. In a small bowl, stir together the cornstarch and 1/4 cup of broth. Add back to the pot and bring to a boil just until thickened, 1 minute. Stir in the sour cream.
7. Pour the sauce over the chicken and sprinkle with parsley to serve.

CHAPTER 3

INDEPENDENT VARIABLES

SIDE DISHES

If I've learned anything during my time at the Worldwide Engineering Brigade, it's that a single change to an equation can alter the outcome of an experiment in unexpected and fascinating ways—and the Pym Test Kitchen has proven that the same rule also applies to meals. Serving a simple sandwich on its own is perfectly fine—especially if it's giant-size!—but add in some loaded tots and you take your lunch to the next level of awesomeness. Then again, you could also go the healthy route and shift the entire feel of the meal by trading in your tots for a sensational side salad. Not really feeling either of those options? Substitute a warm cup of soup straight from Doctor Strange's cauldron (at least I think that's soup) and let it transport you to a whole new dimension of deliciousness! See what I'm going for here? By altering a few simple variables, you open the doors to infinite flavor combinations. These side dishes are a few of my favorites, all of them guaranteed to bring out the best of your Big Bites. Or, if you're really in an experimental mood, feel free to mix and match several scrumptious sides to create a one-of-a-kind mini meal of your own design. The possibilities are endless!

YIELD: 4 SERVINGS

DIFFICULTY: EASY

GALACTIC GREENS

PREP TIME: 10 MIN > COOK TIME: N/A

DRESSING:

1 cup parsley leaves
1 cup cilantro
1/2 cup fresh dill
1/2 cup diced avocado
1/2 cup mayonnaise
1/2 cup sour cream
1 garlic clove
2 tablespoons lemon juice
1 tablespoon white wine vinegar
1 teaspoon Dijon mustard
1/2 teaspoon kosher salt
1/4 teaspoon black pepper

SALAD:

1 large heart of romaine, chopped
1 medium cucumber, sliced
1 cup snap peas
2 green onions, diced

Just beyond the edge of the Avengers Campus sits a terrifying tower owned by some guy named Taneleer Tivan—you may know him better as the Collector. He's basically an eccentric extraterrestrial hoarder who's really into intergalactic oddities. For the first time ever, he's brought his galaxy-spanning collection of rare relics and fantastical flora and fauna to Earth—and it happens to be conveniently on display in our own backyard. If you ask me, the dude is a bit sketchy. I'm relatively convinced he's only here to add a few Avengers to his menagerie . . . but sometimes he lets us play with his telepathic Russian space dog, so I guess he's not all bad. Oh, and occasionally, Mr. Tivan shares some of the unusual produce he's gathered from across the galaxy with the Pym Test Kitchen, adding some otherworldly flair to their recipes. To be fair, not everything has been completely compatible with human taste buds, but this leafy salad was a real breakout success!

INSTRUCTIONS

1. In the base of a blender, add the parsley, cilantro, dill, avocado, mayonnaise, sour cream, garlic, lemon juice, white wine vinegar, Dijon mustard, salt, and pepper. Blend until smooth.
2. In a large bowl, toss romaine, cucumber, and snap peas. Top with green onions and serve with dressing.

V GF

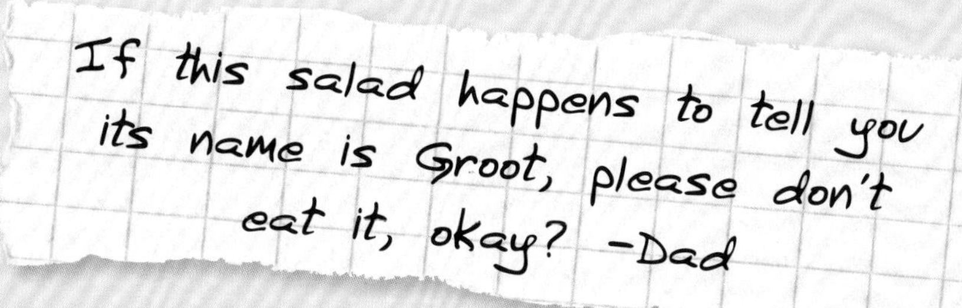

If this salad happens to tell you its name is Groot, please don't eat it, okay? -Dad

YIELD: 1 SERVING

DIFFICULTY: MEDIUM

CAESAR SALAD + COLOSSAL CROUTON

PREP TIME: 15 MIN, ADDITIONAL 24 HOURS > COOK TIME: 25 MIN

The Pym Test Kitchen proudly offers up an endless array of comfort food favorites. But since we're all growing teenagers here at the Worldwide Engineering Brigade, Hope wanted to make sure we had more on our plates than fried chicken and plussed-up PB&Js. I'll admit, when she challenged her team to come up with the perfect side salad, I had my doubts. Not that I have anything against eating healthy, mind you . . . but bowls of limp lettuce aren't all that appetizing to someone like me who's always declared their favorite veggie to be "the crouton." Thankfully, the Pym Test Kitchen solved my sad salad situation with this deconstructed Caesar. It's got hearts of romaine, Kalamata olives, and pickled onions, along with these fun little parmesan crisps and a drizzle of dressing. But the true star of the show is the Colossal Crouton—a huge chunk of garlic-infused, Pym Particle–enhanced bread! You know, maybe a salad at every meal isn't a bad idea after all . . .

PICKLED ONIONS:

- 8 ounces white wine vinegar
- 2 ounces water
- 2½ tablespoons granulated sugar
- 1 teaspoon minced fresh dill
- ½ teaspoon mustard seed
- ¼ teaspoon kosher salt
- 1 garlic clove, minced
- ½ bay leaf
- ¼ cup sliced red onions

PARMESAN CRISPS:

- 3 tablespoons grated Parmesan cheese

CROUTON:

- Blue food coloring
- 1 slice bread
- 1 tablespoon vegetable oil
- 1 tablespoon grated Parmesan cheese
- 1 garlic clove, minced
- 1 teaspoon minced Italian parsley, stemmed
- ⅛ teaspoon black pepper

SALAD:

- 1 heart of romaine, halved
- ¼ cup Caesar dressing
- 1 tablespoon Parmesan cheese
- 5 Kalamata olives
- 1½ tablespoons pickled red onions
- 3 Parmesan crisps

RECIPE CONTINUES ON NEXT PAGE...

INSTRUCTIONS

Make the pickled onions:

1. In a large saucepan, add the white wine vinegar, water, sugar, dill, mustard seed, salt, garlic, and bay leaf and bring to a boil. Lower heat and simmer for 10 minutes. Put the red onions in a bowl, then strain the hot brine through a sieve to cover them. Cover and refrigerate overnight.

Make the Parmesan crisps:

2. Preheat the oven to 400°F. Prep a baking sheet with nonstick foil. Divide the Parmesan cheese into three small piles on the nonstick foil. Flatten slightly. Bake until browned and crispy, 4 minutes. Let cool on the pan. Set aside.

Make the crouton:

3. Preheat oven to 375ºF. Prep a baking sheet with parchment. Use the blue food coloring and a pastry brush to draw a large spiral onto both sides of the bread. Let dry. Once the food coloring is dry, in a small bowl, whisk the vegetable oil, Parmesan cheese, garlic, parsley, stems and black pepper. Spread onto the bread and place on the prepped baking sheet. Bake for 5 minutes. Flip over and cook for another 5 minutes. Set aside.

Make the salad:

4. Place the romaine onto a serving plate. Drizzle the dressing and sprinkle the Parmesan cheese. Add the Kalamata olives, pickled onions, and Parmesan crisps. Place the crouton on top to serve.

YIELD: 24 SERVINGS DIFFICULTY: EASY

COSMIC CHEESE FUSION

PREP TIME: 20 MIN > COOK TIME: 20 MIN

- 2/3 cup whole milk
- 6 tablespoons unsalted butter
- 2 cups tapioca flour
- 1 teaspoon kosher salt
- 1 cup grated Parmesan cheese
- 2 large eggs, lightly beaten

Every once in a while, the Pym Test Kitchen ends up creating a successful recipe completely by accident. While their food science team was busy working out the kinks on the grilled cheeses featured in the Soup and Sandwich Symmetry (Page 67), they experimented with a bunch of different flours and cooking techniques. After accidentally leaving some of their samples in the cosmic-powered convection oven overnight, they returned the next morning to discover that the gluten-free bread and cheese combo had somehow fused together on a molecular scale, resulting in something that was more like a Brazilian pão de queijo than a grilled cheese. Thankfully, they proved their genius-level IQs by being smart enough to taste test their happy mistake instead of just throwing it away. Long story short, these cheesy gluten-free bread bites have since become a fan favorite "off the menu" item that we can't stop snacking on.

INSTRUCTIONS

1. Preheat oven to 375°F. Prep a baking sheet with parchment.
2. In a large saucepan over medium high heat, bring the milk and butter to a boil. Remove from heat and stir in the tapioca flour and salt until smooth. Let cool slightly for 10 minutes.
3. Stir in the cheese and eggs until combined. Drop by 2-tablespoon rounds onto the prepped baking sheet. Bake until lightly browned, 15 to 20 minutes.

V GF

YIELD: 6 SERVINGS

DIFFICULTY: MEDIUM

KINETIC CAULIFLOWER

PREP TIME: 10 MIN > COOK TIME: 25 MIN

2 tablespoons olive oil
1 teaspoon cumin seeds
1 medium onion, diced
2 garlic cloves
1 teaspoon minced fresh ginger
2 small russet potatoes, diced
1 medium cauliflower, cut into small florets
1 large tomato, diced
1 teaspoon coriander
1 teaspoon chili powder
1 teaspoon kosher salt
1/2 teaspoon turmeric
1 teaspoon garam masala
1/4 teaspoon white pepper

One of the first things I remember learning in science class is that there are two basic categories that all types of energy fall into: potential and kinetic. Potential energy is what's stored inside of something, just waiting to burst out. Kinetic energy is active energy, which can manifest in a bunch of forms—like electrical, mechanical, and thermal. In terms of cooking, thermal energy is usually the key. It unlocks the full potential of the foods we eat and transforms raw ingredients into something new and delicious. And I can't think of another veggie that has more natural potential than cauliflower. I've had cauliflower rice, cauliflower pizza crust . . . even a cauliflower steak! But the fragrant blend of spices in this Indian-inspired aloo gobi takes everything good inside of cauliflower and brings it bursting out. And when you tap into potential that strongly, the results can't be defined as anything but kinetic! (Probably.)

INSTRUCTIONS

1. In a large Dutch oven over medium heat, add the olive oil and heat the cumin seeds until fragrant, 1 to 2 minutes. Add the onion, garlic, and ginger, and cook until softened, 2 to 3 minutes.
2. Add the potatoes and cauliflower and cook for 5 to 6 minutes, then add the tomato, coriander, chili powder, salt, turmeric, garam masala, and white pepper. Cover and cook on low for 15 minutes until the potatoes are soft. Serve immediately.

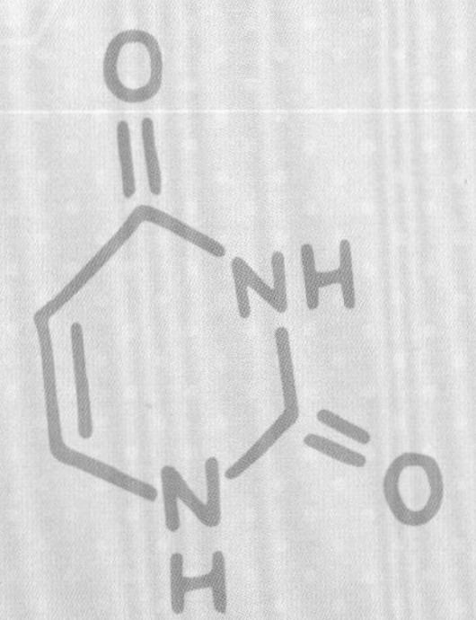

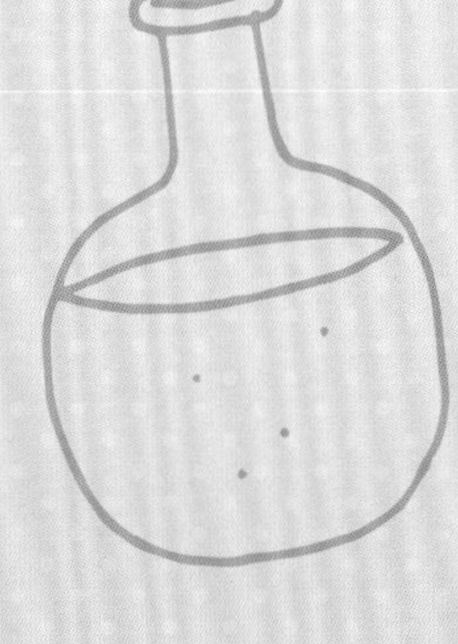

V V+ GF

YIELD: 10 SERVINGS

DIFFICULTY: EASY

HARLEY'S LOCKED & LOADED POTATOES

PREP TIME: 10 MIN > COOK TIME: 35 MIN

POTATOES:

6 slices bacon
32 ounces frozen tater tots
1½ cups shredded cheddar cheese
¼ cup crema or sour cream
¼ cup chopped parsley

FOR SERVING:

½ cup salsa
½ cup guacamole

Hey. I'm Harley Keener. I work with Cassie at the Worldwide Engineering Brigade. My main focus during my time here has been designing the Transport Omni-Drive for the Slinger—our superpowered autonomous vehicle. I'm really proud of my work on it. But for some reason, my scientific contributions keep getting overshadowed by potatoes. (Yeah, you read that right.) At first, it was because I shot Tony Stark with a homemade potato-launching gun the first time we met. But now it's because of a simple side dish that my friends can't seem to get enough of. Honestly, I'm not sure what the big deal is. The Pym Test Kitchen already serves Crispy Potato Bites with some of their mega-size meals. I just took those and added some melted cheese, crumbled bacon, and sour cream. It's not rocket science, but I guess it is pretty tasty . . . which is good, because I get the strange feeling that this is the invention I'm going to be remembered for most!

INSTRUCTIONS

1. In a large skillet over medium-high heat, cook the bacon for 8 to 10 minutes until crispy. Roughly chop, then set aside.
2. Preheat oven to 425°F. Arrange the tater tots on a parchment-lined baking sheet and bake for 20 minutes until golden brown.
3. Sprinkle the cheese over the tots, then return to oven for another 5 minutes until the cheese has melted.
4. Add the bacon on top. Drizzle the crema over it and sprinkle the parsley. Serve with salsa and guacamole on the side.

I'm sure you'll have a potato-free breakthrough someday, Harley! Ever consider eggplants?
-Peter

YIELD: 6 SERVINGS

DIFFICULTY: MEDIUM

DOCTOR STRANGE'S BUBBLING CAULDRON

PREP TIME: 20 MIN > COOK TIME: 30 MIN

PARMESAN PORTALS:

1 cup grated Parmesan cheese

SOUP:

6 slices bacon, diced
2 tablespoons unsalted butter
1 medium onion, diced
2 stalks celery, diced
32 ounces chicken broth
2 potatoes, peeled and diced
One 16-oz bag frozen corn
1½ teaspoons kosher salt
½ teaspoon garlic powder
½ teaspoon paprika
½ teaspoon black pepper
½ teaspoon onion powder
1 cup heavy cream
2 tablespoons cornstarch

Right across from the Worldwide Engineering Brigade Workshop is this peaceful little park with a whole lot of history. Apparently, it's always been the site of unexplained events and weird energies. When the Avengers Campus opened, Doctor Strange reversed some super-secret spells and revealed the ruins of the Ancient Sanctum—a mystical nexus point with doors that open to just about anywhere you can imagine! Sometimes they lead to a monastery in Kamar-Taj. Other times it's the Dark Dimension. But the best destination is always the kitchen of the Sanctum Sanctorum in NYC. Strange is always cooking up something in his cauldron, but it's usually potions made with bat tongues or newt eyes or whatever. When the Doc is off saving other dimensions, though, his pal Wong takes over and cooks up this great gluten-free corn chowder (with Parmesan crisps that look like teeny spell discs). This supreme soup may not actually be magical, but it sure tastes like it is!

INSTRUCTIONS

Make the Parmesan portals:

1. Preheat the oven to 400°F. Prep a baking sheet with nonstick foil. Divide the Parmesan cheese into four swirls onto the nonstick foil. Flatten slightly. Bake until browned and crispy, 4 to 5 minutes. Let cool on the pan. Set aside.

Make the soup:

2. In a large pot over medium heat, cook the bacon until crisp, 7 to 8 minutes. Remove and pour out half the bacon grease.
3. In the same pot, add the butter, onions, and celery, cooking until soft, 3 to 4 minutes.
4. Add the chicken broth. Add the potatoes and bring to a boil. Reduce to a simmer and cook until the potatoes are tender, 10 minutes.
5. Add the corn, salt, garlic powder, paprika, pepper, and onion powder. Stir in the heavy cream and add the bacon back into the pot.
6. In a small bowl, stir the cornstarch with 2 tablespoons of broth to make a slurry. Stir the slurry back into the pot, and simmer for another 5 to 7 minutes.
7. Ladle the soup into bowls and top with Parmesan portals to serve.

GF

YIELD: 6 SERVINGS | DIFFICULTY: EASY

BIFROST FRUIT SALAD

PREP TIME: 20 MIN > COOK TIME: N/A

DRESSING:

1⁄3 cup extra virgin olive oil
1⁄2 cup orange juice
1 tablespoon lime juice
1 tablespoon honey
1 teaspoon orange zest

FRUIT:

1 cup strawberries
1 cup raspberries
1 cup diced cantaloupe
1 cup mandarin oranges
1 cup diced pineapple
1 cup diced mango
1 cup diced kiwi
1 cup green grapes
1 cup blueberries
1 cup purple grapes

Health experts are always saying that you should try to "eat the rainbow" to get the widest variety of fruits and veggies in your daily diet. But when you're friends with honest-to-goodness Asgardian gods, why not "eat the Rainbow Bridge" instead? Okay, so maybe this fruit salad isn't literally made from part of the legendary Bifrost. (That would be crazy.) But it does include some of the freshest produce the Nine Realms have to offer. If you've never had berries picked fresh from the banks of Honeywine Falls in Alfheim, you're missing out! This salad was originally served at a banquet that Thor hosted at Avengers HQ on some random Thursday. Now, whenever we're craving this epic blend of fruity flavors, we just yell as loud as we can and hope that Heimdall is listening (which he always is). When he's not in the mood to make a delivery (which he almost never is), normal Midgardian (a.k.a. Earth) fruit works just fine, too.

INSTRUCTIONS

1. In a medium bowl, whisk together the olive oil, orange juice, lime juice, honey, and orange zest. Set aside.
2. On a large serving dish, lay out each fruit by color. Serve with dressing.

V GF

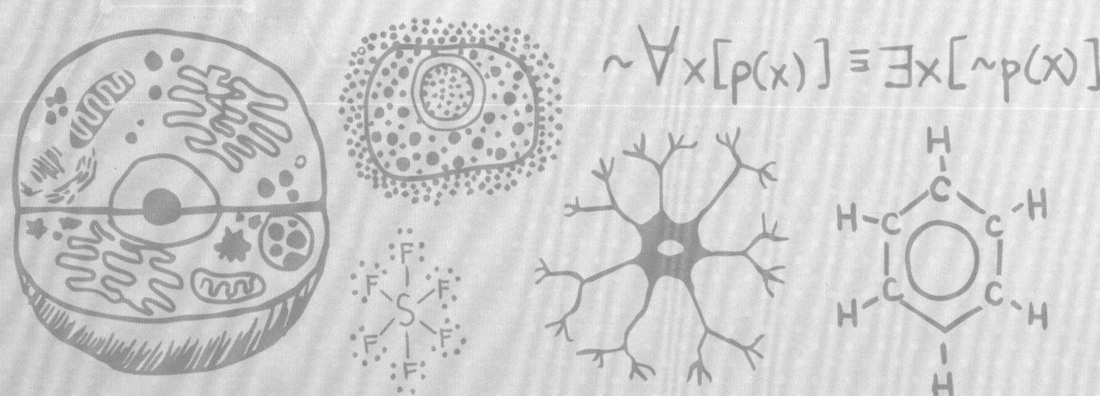

YIELD: 6 SERVINGS DIFFICULTY: EASY

FORMIDABLE FRITES

PREP TIME: 5 MIN > COOK TIME: 20 MIN

24 ounces frozen French fries
Olive oil spray
1 tablespoon black truffle oil
1/4 cup furikake seasoning
1/4 cup grated Parmesan cheese
1 teaspoon salt

With all the weird and wild experimental eats dished out at the Pym Test Kitchen each and every day, there's a pretty good chance no one would complain if they served up their supersize sandwiches with a plentiful pile of plain old potatoes. Not every component of the meal has to push food science in bold new directions, right? Wrong. Even their French fries are put through rigorous trials to determine everything from the precise dimensions of salt crystals to which test batch of ketchup is the ideal match (the answer is #MP471979). Once they've established a proper foundation, that's when the Pym team starts to get creative and play with other possibilities. These frites tossed in truffle oil, Parmesan cheese, and furikake (a savory seaweed-based seasoning) are a perfect example of how something as familiar as a French fry can be elevated to whole new heights without wasting a single Pym Particle!

INSTRUCTIONS

1. Preheat the oven to 425°F. Prep a baking sheet with parchment or a silicon baking mat.
2. Spread the fries evenly onto the pan and spray them with olive oil. Bake for 20 minutes until crisp and browned.
3. In a large bowl, toss the hot fries with truffle oil, furikake, Parmesan cheese, and salt. Serve immediately.

V GF

Someone else perfected a potato dish?
Harley might be out of a job...
-Peter

PYM
TEST KITCHE

YIELD: 8 SERVINGS DIFFICULTY: DIFFICULT

MACROSCOPIC MAC & CHEESE

PREP TIME: 15 MIN > COOK TIME: 40 MIN

MACARONI:

24 ounces jumbo shell pasta
1/2 cup (1 stick) unsalted butter, melted
1/2 cup all-purpose flour
3 cups whole milk
1 cup heavy cream
2 teaspoons dry mustard
1 1/2 teaspoons garlic powder
1 teaspoon paprika
1 teaspoon kosher salt
1 teaspoon white pepper
1/2 teaspoon garlic salt
4 cups shredded sharp cheddar cheese

TOPPING:

1 cup panko breadcrumbs
1 cup cheese crackers, crushed
6 tablespoons unsalted butter, melted

You would think that making macaroni and cheese would be easy. (Come on! Both ingredients are listed right there in the name!) But even the most straightforward culinary combinations can have an endless number of variations. Some folks like their macaroni baked, while others prefer it boiled. Cheese can range from gooey and stringy to smooth and creamy. Whether you get yours at a trendy local gastropub or straight out of a box, the number of potential deviations (and opinions) makes defining a "perfect" mac & cheese seem scientifically impossible. But after a wide-ranging study involving a test group of 1,000 participants ranging from ages 3 to 93, the Pym Test Kitchen has come pretty darn close! This proprietary formula features a crisp topping to evoke that traditional homemade feel but counters it with gigantified shell noodles to offer a modern twist. It's the best of both worlds . . . but, really, what mac & cheese isn't?

INSTRUCTIONS >>>>>>>

Make the macaroni:

1. In a large pot, boil water and cook the pasta according to directions. Drain but do not rinse.
2. Preheat the oven to 350°F. Prep a deep 9-by-13-inch baking dish with nonstick spray. Set aside.
3. In a Dutch oven over medium-high, add the melted butter and whisk in the flour for one minute until lightly browned. Whisk in the milk and heavy cream for 1 to 2 minutes until bubbling.
4. Stir in the mustard, garlic powder, paprika, salt, white pepper, and garlic salt. Whisk in the cheese one cup at a time until smooth.
5. Stir in the cooked pasta, tossing to coat. Pour into the prepped baking dish.

Make the topping:

6. In a small bowl stir together the panko, cheese crackers, and melted butter. Sprinkle on top and bake until browned and bubbly, 25 minutes.

YIELD: 6 SERVINGS | DIFFICULTY: EASY

QUANTUM ENTANGLED NOODLE SALAD

PREP TIME: 10 MIN > COOK TIME: N/A

There's no easy way to describe quantum entanglement. (Just listen to my dad try to explain it and I promise you'll agree!) It's basically when two particles are so inherently connected to each other that you can't define one without the other. It's actually kind of sweet when you think about it. I mean, some things are just meant to go together, and you can't imagine them ever being apart. That's kinda how I feel about this noodle salad. All of the components, from the ramen noodles to the crunchy cabbage, are so essential to the mix that you can't even fathom how they could ever exist without each other. Now, anytime I eat cabbage, I automatically think of ramen. Whenever I'm slurping ramen, I wish I had some cabbage. Maybe it's just because this is a really good recipe and nothing more, but as with all things that come out of the Pym Test Kitchen, I blame science!

SALAD:

3 cups shredded green cabbage
1 cup shredded red cabbage
1/2 cup grated carrots
1/2 cup diced cucumbers
2 green onions, minced
1/2 cup sliced almonds
1 package ramen noodles, crushed (discard the seasoning packet)

DRESSING:

1/4 cup vegetable oil
3 tablespoons white vinegar
1 tablespoon packed light brown sugar
1 teaspoon sesame oil
1 teaspoon soy sauce
1/2 teaspoon black pepper

INSTRUCTIONS >>>>>

1. In a large bowl, toss the green cabbage, red cabbage, carrots, and cucumbers. Sprinkle the green onions, almonds, and ramen noodles. Set aside.
2. In a sealable jar, add the vegetable oil, vinegar, brown sugar, sesame oil, soy sauce, and pepper. Drizzle the dressing over the salad and serve.

YIELD: 4 SERVINGS DIFFICULTY: EASY

WASP'S STINGING CORN COBS

PREP TIME: 10 MIN > COOK TIME: 40 MIN

4 ears fresh corn, in husks
1/2 cup honey
2 teaspoons red pepper flakes
1 teaspoon Shichimi togarashi

It's no secret that my dad is constantly trying to impress Hope. But I'm not sure if naming this side dish after her super hero alter ego earned him any points. Don't get me wrong, it's a fantastic corn on the cob recipe that gets its signature "sting" from a drizzle of hot honey. But that's where things go a bit off the rails . . . because the majority of species of wasps don't actually produce honey at all! My dad should be no stranger to this fact (you know, since he can literally talk to insects via that high-tech helmet of his). But I guess scientific accuracy is an afterthought when trying to win over (checks notes) the head of a major scientific research company?! Oof. Anyway, while the name might be a touch off-brand, the taste here is completely on point. At least you'll be feeling the sting for all the right reasons . . . unlike my dad.

INSTRUCTIONS

1. Preheat the oven to 375°F. Place the corn directly onto the oven rack and cook for 30 minutes.
2. In a small saucepan over medium-low heat, add the honey, red pepper flakes, and togarashi. Bring to a simmer, then remove from heat and let cool slightly.
3. To serve, pull the husks back and drizzle the hot honey over the corn.

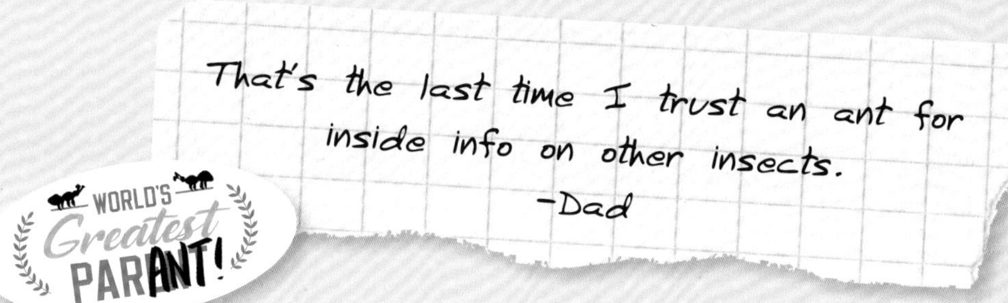

That's the last time I trust an ant for
inside info on other insects.
-Dad
WORLD'S
Greatest
PARANT!

V GF

PYM
TEST KITCHEN

YIELD: 8 SERVINGS DIFFICULTY: EASY

QUANTIFIED STUDY OF CHILI

PREP TIME: 15 MIN > COOK TIME: 40 MIN

1 tablespoon olive oil
1 medium onion, diced (reserve 2 tablespoons for garnish)
2 garlic cloves, minced
1 pound ground beef
One 14-ounce can diced tomatoes
One 8-ounce can tomato sauce
2 tablespoons chili powder
2 teaspoons packed light brown sugar
2 teaspoons cumin
1 teaspoon garlic salt
1 teaspoon onion powder
1 teaspoon oregano
1/4 teaspoon black pepper
1 cup shredded cheddar cheese
1 teaspoon chopped parsley
Tortilla chips, for serving

This summer, the Avengers Campus was home to the "First Annual Pym Test Kitchen Chili Cook-Off!" Simultaneously, it was also home to the "Last Annual Pym Test Kitchen Chili Cook-Off!" (since the entire thing was kind of a disaster). What was supposed to be a single afternoon of food and fun ended up stretching out into twenty-seven hours of deep critical analysis. Scoville Heat Units were measured, and olfactory reactions were closely monitored and recorded. Meanwhile, a bunch of hungry kids from the lab next door (that's us!) stared longingly with spoons in their hands and nothing in their stomachs. When the waiting was finally over, the winner was unanimous—a warm, savory chili-cheese dip served with crunchy tortilla chips. It defied all the expectations of a standard chili but checked all the boxes when it came to flavor. I'm honestly not sure if any food is worth that kind of wait . . . but if anything comes close, it's this!

INSTRUCTIONS

1. Preheat oven to 350°F.
2. In a skillet over medium-high heat, add olive oil and cook the onion (minus two tablespoons) and garlic until soft, 5 to 6 minutes. Add the ground beef and cook until browned, 5 to 7 minutes.
3. Add the diced tomatoes, tomato sauce, chili powder, brown sugar, cumin, garlic salt, onion powder, oregano, and black pepper. Simmer on low for 20 minutes.
4. Pour into an 8 x 8 baking dish. Top with cheese and bake until the cheese is melted, 10 minutes.
5. Top with reserved onions and parsley. Serve with chips.

CHAPTER 4

CONFECTIONARY CONCLUSIONS

DESSERTS

After all the astounding things I've witnessed on the Avengers Campus, I don't believe in many absolutes anymore. But this one still stands: If you don't love dessert, we can't be friends. Sorry (not sorry). But seriously, no matter what adults may try to tell you, dessert is the only reason to ever finish your meal (especially if Brussels sprouts are involved). While my dad and I are totally on the same page about this, the Pym Test Kitchen is a bit more focused on the type of serious food science that doesn't instantly induce sugar shock. So, while I can convince them to supersize me a cookie or a Choco-Smash Candy Bar every now and then, I've been forced to seek out other creative solutions to satisfy my sweet tooth this summer. Lucky for me, finding creative solutions is exactly why the Worldwide Engineering Brigade was formed! My new friends were always more than glad to take a break from building a better tomorrow if it meant making right this moment just a teeny bit yummier. I mean, who would've thought the same laboratory oven we used to synthesize Vibranium alloys would also make perfect batch of brownies? These desserts may have different origins, but they all lead to the exact same result: a smile.

YIELD: 12 SERVINGS — DIFFICULTY: MEDIUM

PEACH PYM PIES

PREP TIME: 10 MIN > COOK TIME: 25 MIN

4 cups diced fresh peaches
1/2 cup packed light brown sugar
1/4 cup granulated sugar
3 tablespoons cornstarch
2 teaspoons lemon juice
1 teaspoon vanilla extract
1/2 teaspoon cinnamon
1/4 teaspoon kosher salt
4 tablespoons unsalted butter, diced
2 discs premade pie dough
1 large egg plus 1 tablespoon water, for egg wash

SPECIAL SUPPLIES:
Round cookie cutter

Coming from a blended family, I know it's completely normal to miss one parent when you're staying with the other. But when Dad got lost in the Quantum Realm for a few years . . . well, let's just say I needed as much comfort as I could get. Hope says she knows exactly how I felt, since her mom, Janet van Dyne, got stranded in that same subatomic dimension back when Hope was just a kid. I guess her dad didn't offer much emotional support, so Hope had to find ways to pull herself through. One of the ways she coped was by baking her mom's old recipes. This peach pie recipe in particular was one that Hope said made her feel like her mom was still there with her even while she was gone. These petite pies may earn the "Pym" in their name from the fact that they're miniaturized using Pym Particles, but this recipe is dedicated to some of the strongest women I know—the van Dynes.

INSTRUCTIONS

1. Preheat the oven to 400°F. Prep a muffin tin with nonstick spray.
2. In a large bowl, toss the peaches, brown sugar, granulated sugar, cornstarch, lemon juice, vanilla, cinnamon, and salt. Set aside.
3. Onto a floured surface, roll out half the dough into a circle 1/8-inch thick. Use a 5-inch cutter to cut circles, then lightly press them into the prepped muffin tin. Top with spoonfuls of filling and the diced butter.
4. Roll out the remaining dough into another circle 1/8-inch thick and cut into 1/4-inch strips. Use the strips to create lattice patterns over the filling. Brush with egg wash.
5. Bake for 20 to 25 minutes until the crust is browned and the filling is bubbly. Let the pies cool, then run a knife around the edges to remove from the pan and serve.

I COULDN'T BE MORE HONORED, CASSIE. (THIS IS SO MUCH BETTER THAN CORN COBS.)
-HOPE

YIELD: 6 SERVINGS

DIFFICULTY: DIFFICULT

CELESTIAL-SIZE CHOCO-SMASH SUNDAE

PREP TIME: 40 MIN, ADDITIONAL 8 HOURS FOR FREEZING > COOK TIME: 40 MIN

When your lab is funded by mega-conglomerates, you have to work extra hard to make sure that your research remains unbiased. You never want someone to think the results of your studies were skewed in favor of the organizations subsidizing them. But while that may require an added layer of vigilance on our part, there are some definite perks to corporate sponsorship that balance it all out. For instance, one of the Worldwide Engineering Brigade's financial backers happens to have a confections division that makes the popular Choco-Smash Candy Bar . . . which means our vending machine is always fully stocked! Even so, it's hard to get enough of this killer combo of dark chocolate, peanuts, caramel, nougat, and chocolate brownie. Since I won't have the team at the Pym Test Kitchen on hand to "Celestial-size" one whenever my hunger Hulks out, I came up with this recipe that captures all of the same addictive flavors in sundae form!

PEANUT BUTTER ICE CREAM:

One 14-ounce can sweetened condensed milk
1/2 cup smooth peanut butter
1/2 teaspoon salt
1 teaspoon vanilla
2 cups heavy whipping cream

PEANUT BUTTER MOUSSE:

1/2 cup creamy peanut butter
1/3 cup chopped white chocolate, melted
1/4 teaspoon kosher salt

BROWNIE:

1 cup (2 sticks) unsalted butter
1/2 cup chopped dark chocolate
3/4 cup packed light brown sugar
1/2 cup granulated sugar
3 large eggs
1 teaspoon vanilla extract
1 cup all-purpose flour
1/4 cup cocoa powder
1/2 teaspoon kosher salt

FOR SERVING:

1/4 cup caramel sauce
1/4 cup chocolate sauce
1/2 cup whipped cream
1/4 cup roasted peanuts

INSTRUCTIONS

Make the ice cream:

1. In a large bowl, use a hand mixer to stir together the sweetened condensed milk, peanut butter, salt, and vanilla until just combined. Stir in the heavy whipping cream, mixing well. Pour into a 5-by-9-inch loaf pan and cover with plastic wrap. Freeze until firm, 6 to 8 hours.

Make the mousse:

2. In a small bowl, warm the peanut butter in the microwave for 15 seconds until softened. In a medium bowl, use a hand mixer to stir together the softened peanut butter, melted white chocolate, and salt until smooth, 2 to 3 minutes. Pour into a shallow pan to cool. Place a piece of plastic wrap directly onto the surface of the mousse and set aside.

Make the brownie:

3. Preheat the oven to 350°F. Prep an 8-by-8-inch pan lined with parchment and greased with nonstick spray.
4. In a double boiler over medium heat, combine the butter and dark chocolate, stirring until melted. Take off heat and let cool slightly. Set aside.
5. In a large bowl, stir together the brown sugar and granulated sugar. Pour over the butter mixture and stir until combined.
6. Stir in the eggs and vanilla until just combined. Add in the flour, cocoa powder, and salt, stirring until smooth. Pour into the prepped pan. Bake until just cooked, 30 to 40 minutes. Let cool completely.

To serve:

7. Remove the brownie from the pan and place onto a serving platter. Spoon the mousse into a pastry bag and pipe onto the brownie. Scoop the peanut butter ice cream and place on top of the mousse. Drizzle the caramel sauce and chocolate sauce over it and top with whipped cream. Sprinkle over the peanuts. Cut into six pieces, to serve.

YIELD: 4 SERVINGS DIFFICULTY: MEDIUM

COSMIC CREAM PARFAIT

PREP TIME: 40 MIN > COOK TIME: 5 MIN

The Pym Test Kitchen regularly delivers healthy servings of amazement and disbelief, thanks to the unique juxtapositions of sizes and flavors they've managed to produce. With such unprecedented presentation, it's easy to forget that most of their recipes were designed to use everyday ingredients at unusual scales. When we're looking for flavors that are truly out of this world, we head on over to Taneleer Tivan's Terran Treats—a small food stall stationed in front of Tivan's collection of interstellar curiosities that offers a selection of snacks curated specifically for "Terran" (better known as "human") customers. I've never tasted anything quite like their Cosmic Cream Orb. And since I honestly don't have a clue what this thing actually is or what galaxy it came from, there's no way for me to bake my own at home. But the raspberry cream in this parfait comes pretty close to capturing the essence of this decadent dessert, whatever it is.

RASPBERRY PUREE:

6 ounces raspberries
1/4 cup granulated sugar
1 tablespoon lemon juice

RASPBERRY CREAM:

One 0.25-ounce envelope powdered gelatin
1/4 cup water
1/2 cup heavy cream
8 ounces cream cheese
1/4 cup sour cream
1/3 cup powdered sugar
1/2 teaspoon orange juice
1/2 teaspoon lemon juice
1/2 teaspoon vanilla extract
purple food gel dye, as needed

FOR SERVING:

2 cups crumbled chocolate cookies
1 cup whipped cream
4 raspberries, for serving
4 mint leaves, for serving

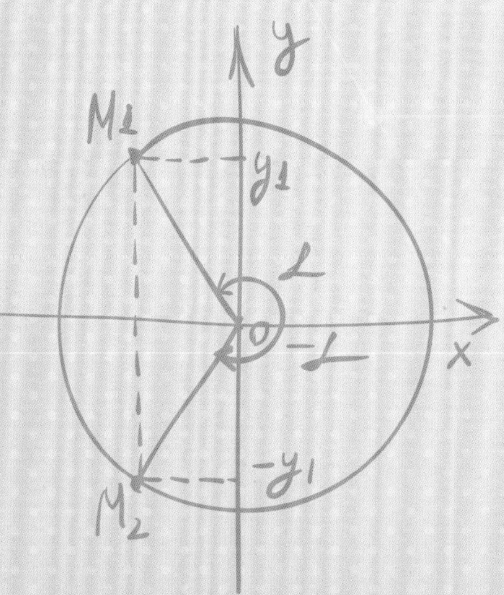

INSTRUCTIONS >>>>>

Make the puree:

1. In a large saucepan over medium heat, add the raspberries, sugar, and lemon juice. Bring to a boil. Lower the heat and let simmer for 5 minutes. Strain through a sieve and let cool completely.

Make the cream:

2. In a small bowl, sprinkle the gelatin over the water and let bloom. Set aside.
3. In a large bowl, use a handheld mixer to whip the heavy cream, cream cheese, sour cream, powdered sugar, orange juice, lemon juice, and vanilla.
4. Stir in the purple food gel dye, gelatin, and the raspberry puree. Let set in the refrigerator for 30 minutes.

To serve:

5. Pipe the cream mixture into four small serving glasses, alternating layers with crumbled cookies.
6. Top with whipped cream, more crumbled cookies, a raspberry, and a mint leaf.

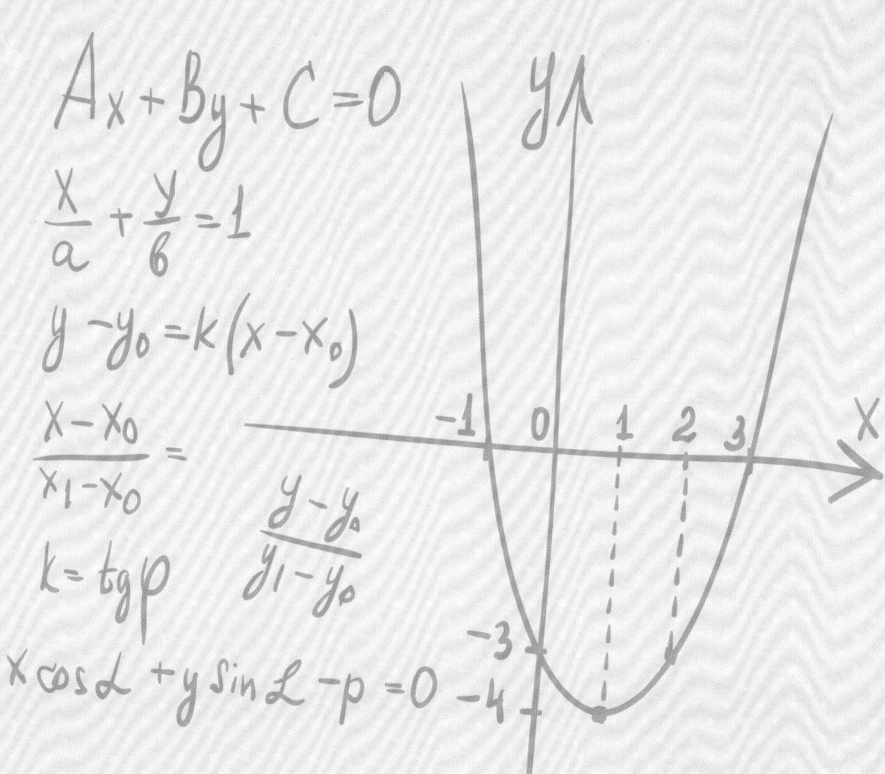

YIELD: 4 SERVINGS

DIFFICULTY: MEDIUM

TRANSCENDENTAL TERRAN SPIRALS

PREP TIME: 30 MIN > COOK TIME: 10 MIN

3/4 cup water
1/4 cup pineapple juice
1/2 cup (1 stick) unsalted butter
1 tablespoon granulated sugar
1 cup all-purpose flour
2 tablespoons crushed pineapple, well drained
1/2 teaspoon cinnamon
1/4 teaspoon salt
1/2 teaspoon clear vanilla
Green food gel dye
3 large eggs
1 quart vegetable oil, for frying

SUGAR:
1/2 cup granulated sugar
1 teaspoon cinnamon

The Terran Treats stand in front of Taneleer Tivan's museum is a favorite snacking spot for us at the Worldwide Engineering Brigade, but we always try to stay on full alert whenever the "Collector" himself is lurking around. It's clear that guy has intentions other than sharing the flavors of the galaxy with us . . . and I don't think I want to be the one who finds out what they actually are. I mean, Star-Lord and his crew went into his tower a couple weeks back, and I haven't seen them since! (Someone really ought to look into that.) I suppose extraterrestrial eats as good as this one—which is some sort of weird green pastry that looks like a cinnamon roll but tastes like a pineapple churro—are worth a little risk. But while my mouth will be full, my head will be on a swivel—because even though these desserts are delectable, I doubt they'd taste nearly as good if I was eating them while on display in a weird alien zoo.

INSTRUCTIONS

1. In a small saucepan over medium heat, add water, pineapple juice, butter, and sugar. Bring to a boil and remove from heat, then quickly stir in the flour. Let cool for 10 minutes.
2. Transfer to the bowl of an electric mixer. Set speed to 2, then stir in the crushed pineapple, cinnamon, salt, clear vanilla, and green food gel dye. Stir in the eggs one at a time.
3. Place batter into a pastry bag fitted with a large star tip. Pipe four large spirals onto parchment paper. Place in the freezer for 20 minutes.
4. In a large Dutch oven, heat oil to 350°F. Fry the spirals for 3 minutes on each side until crispy and cooked through. Let drain on a wire rack.
5. In a shallow dish, whisk the sugar and cinnamon. While still warm, toss the spirals in the mixture to coat.

YIELD: 10 SERVINGS

DIFFICULTY: MEDIUM

MULTIVERSAL MULTILAYERED FROZEN ORB

PREP TIME: 4 HOURS > COOK TIME: N/A

- 1 half gallon rainbow sherbet, softened
- 1 half gallon softened vanilla ice cream, divided
- 2 pints lime sherbet, softened
- 2 pints raspberry sorbet, softened

On occasion, the enchanted doors of the Ancient Sanctum open to reveal a passageway to a mountain monastery in Kamar-Taj. Doctor Strange took us on a field trip there once to see the place where he learned humility (I think it's still a work in progress) and began his journey to become the Sorcerer Supreme. While we were there, we got to look thorough their amazing library full of ancient tomes. And while most of the spellbooks were off-limits to us, they had a surprising selection of cookbooks on those dusty old shelves. One of them—the Cookbook of Cagliostro—included a recipe for this multilayered ice cream bombe, which kinda reminded us all of that weird, mystical orb in the middle of the Sanctum's courtyard. You know, the one that starts glowing every night for reasons that none of us have been able to figure out yet? Anyway, conjuring up a dessert like this would add a touch of extra magic to any special occasion!

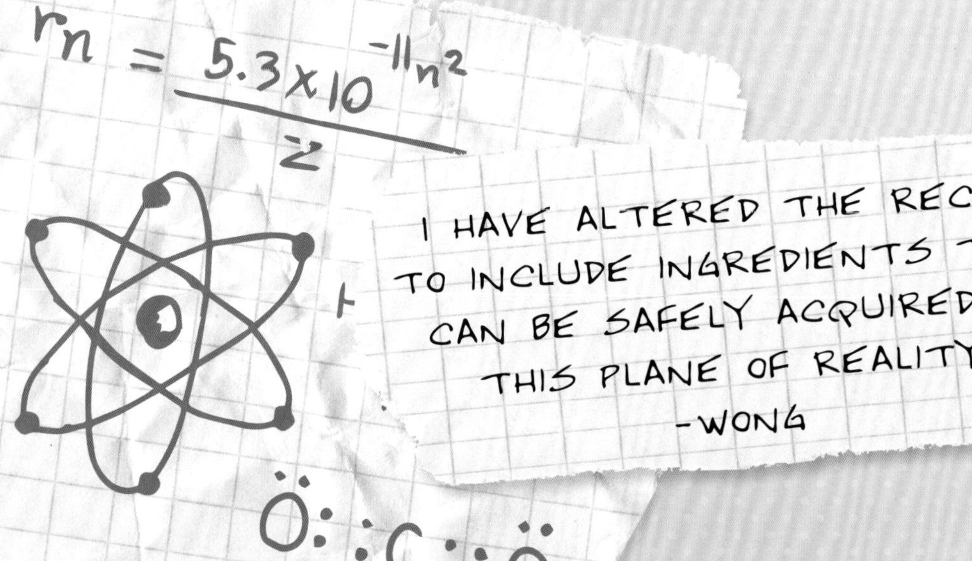

rn = 5.3x10^-11 n^2 / Z
I HAVE ALTERED THE RECIPE TO INCLUDE INGREDIENTS THAT CAN BE SAFELY ACQUIRED IN THIS PLANE OF REALITY.
-WONG
O::C::O

V GF

INSTRUCTIONS

1. Line a large bowl with plastic wrap and let the edges overhang.
2. Use a spatula to spread the rainbow sherbet around the inside of the bowl. Freeze until firm, 1 hour.
3. Spread half the vanilla ice cream in a thin, even layer on top of the rainbow sherbet. Freeze for 45 minutes.
4. Spread the lime sherbet over the vanilla layer, then freeze for 45 minutes.
5. Finally, fill the center of the bombe with the raspberry sorbet. Spread the remaining vanilla on top to cover completely. Freeze until firm.
6. Place a warm towel around the bowl and use the plastic wrap to pull out the bombe. Place on a serving plate and cut into wedges.

YIELD: 8 SERVINGS DIFFICULTY: DIFFICULT

LUNELLA'S MOON PIES

PREP TIME: 1 HOUR > COOK TIME: 15 MIN

COOKIES:

1 cup graham cracker crumbs
3/4 cup all-purpose flour
1/2 teaspoon baking powder
1/2 teaspoon cinnamon
1/4 teaspoon kosher salt
4 tablespoons unsalted butter, softened
2/3 cup packed light brown sugar
1 large egg
1/2 teaspoon vanilla extract
1 cup marshmallow crème

GLAZE:

18 ounces dark chocolate, chopped
1 tablespoon unsalted butter

Hi! My name's Lunella Lafayette. I'm the youngest engineer here at the Worldwide Engineering Brigade (WEB), but that doesn't mean I'm any less important to the team. Even though I'm a genius, I'm also still just a kid . . . so being away from home for the whole summer to work on the targeting and vision system for Project Slinger was a little scary sometimes. Cassie was like a big sister to me, which helped a lot. But when I was really missing home, I put down my nuclear-powered screwdriver and picked up a spatula instead to whip up a batch of my Grandma JoJo's famous Moon Pies. I love these things almost as much as I love science (but not quite as much as I love dinosaurs). One bite of these cream-filled, chocolate-dipped cookies instantly makes me feel like I'm back on the Lower East Side surrounded by family. And now that I get to share them with my new family—like Cassie and all my other friends at WEB—I'm simply over the moon! (Get it?)

INSTRUCTIONS >>>>>>>>

Make the cookies:

1. Preheat the oven to 350°F. Prep baking sheets with parchment paper.
2. In a large bowl, whisk the graham cracker crumbs, flour, baking powder, cinnamon, and salt. Set aside.
3. In the bowl of an electric mixer, cream the butter and brown sugar until fluffy, 3 to 4 minutes. Stir in the egg and vanilla until combined. Fold in the dry ingredients until just combined.
4. On a floured surface, roll out the dough to 1/4-inch thick. Use a 2 1/4-inch round cutter to cut out 16 circles. Place circles onto the prepped baking sheets and bake for 10 minutes until golden brown. Let cool on a wire rack.
5. Spoon 1 to 2 tablespoons marshmallow crème onto half of the cooled cookies. Top with a second cookie to sandwich. Repeat with the rest of the cookies and place in the freezer for 15 to 20 minutes.

Make the glaze:

6. In a double boiler, melt the dark chocolate and stir in the butter.
7. Pour the chocolate into a medium bowl. Dip the cookies into the chocolate, then place onto a parchment-lined baking sheet.
8. Once the chocolate has set, the cookies are ready to serve.

YIELD: 12 SERVINGS | DIFFICULTY: MEDIUM

DOREEN'S NUTTY BROWNIES

PREP TIME: 10 MIN > COOK TIME: 20 MIN

1 cup semisweet chocolate, chopped
1/2 cup (1 stick) unsalted butter
1 cup granulated sugar
1 teaspoon vanilla extract
3 large eggs
1/2 cup all-purpose flour
1/3 cup cocoa powder
12 peanut butter cups

Oh, wow. Cassie asked me to contribute something to her collection of recipes and memories . . . but where do I even start? Umm, let's see . . . my name is Doreen. Doreen Allene Green. I got recruited as an engineer at the Worldwide Engineering Brigade thanks to my sweet computer programming skills. I developed an autonomous open-source artificial intelligence for our lab and the Slinger vehicles. (Its name is S.H.A.R.I.N.) When I'm not busy "doing the science," I'm usually eating nuts and kicking butts as the unbeatable—wait, I probably shouldn't put that part in writing. Hmm . . . Oh! I love squirrels! My best friend is one named Tippy-Toe. Sometimes, after a long day of definitely not fighting crime, I like to bake Tippy a batch of my favorite brownies. The secret ingredient is a full peanut butter cup right in the middle! You don't need to have a bushy tail and furry little ears to go nuts for this treat . . . but can you imagine how adorable that would look?

INSTRUCTIONS >>>>>>>>

1. Preheat oven to 350°F. Prep a cupcake pan with liners.
2. In a double boiler, melt the chocolate chips and the butter, stirring constantly. Once melted and combined, carefully take off the heat and let cool for a few minutes.
3. Whisk in the sugar until smooth. Quickly add the vanilla and eggs, whisking constantly. Stir in the flour and cocoa, whisking just until combined.
4. Spoon 1 tablespoon of batter into each liner. Place one peanut butter cup on top, then add more batter, covering the cookie completely.
5. Bake for 20 minutes. Let cool on a wire rack.

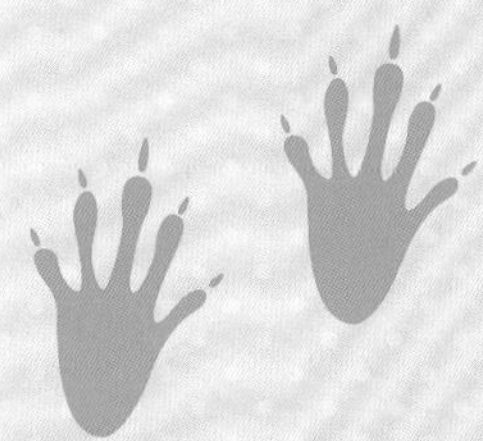

YIELD: 24 SERVINGS DIFFICULTY: MEDIUM

MOLECULAR MOCHI MUNCHIES

PREP TIME: 5 MIN > COOK TIME: 5 MIN

COATING:

1/2 cup granulated sugar
1 tablespoon cinnamon

DONUTS:

2 cups mochiko (sweet rice flour)
3/4 cup granulated sugar
2 tablespoons baking powder
1/2 teaspoon cinnamon
1/4 teaspoon nutmeg
1 cup whole milk
1 large egg
1 teaspoon vanilla extract
1 quart vegetable oil, for frying

When the team at the Worldwide Engineering Brigade Workshop wants to study a scientific reaction on a molecular level, you might assume that we'd take advantage of the unlimited supply of Pym Particles readily available right next door at the Pym Test Kitchen. But as anyone who's been shrunk down to subatomic size only to become unmoored in time and space might tell you, it's way too dangerous to take that kind of risk unless absolutely necessary. Instead, we map out our molecular models using a slightly more traditional—and entirely more edible—means. Using batches of these chewy little donut holes to represent the atoms, we build simple ball-and-spoke-style simulations that help us figure out exactly how the complex bonds are likely to form. And since all our research has, like, twelve levels of NDAs attached to it, we get to eat all of the evidence when our top-secret projects have come to a close!

INSTRUCTIONS >>>>>

1. In a small bowl stir together the sugar and cinnamon. Set aside.
2. In a large bowl, whisk together the mochiko, sugar, baking powder, cinnamon, and nutmeg.
3. Make a well in the center of the dry ingredients and stir in the milk, egg, and vanilla until just combined.
4. In a Dutch oven, heat the oil to 350°F. Drop the dough by the tablespoon into the oil. Once the dough floats, fry for 2 to 3 minutes on each side until golden brown. Let drain slightly on a wire rack, and while the donuts are still hot, roll in the cinnamon sugar mixture. Serve immediately.

I HAD NO IDEA THE ATOMIC STRUCTURE OF VIBRANIUM WOULD TASTE SO DELIGHTFUL.
-ONOME

V GF

YIELD: 10 SERVINGS DIFFICULTY: EASY

MEGA CEREAL TREATS

PREP TIME: 10 MIN > COOK TIME: 5 MIN

3 tablespoons unsalted butter
One 10-ounce package marshmallows
$^1/_2$ teaspoon vanilla
$^1/_4$ teaspoon kosher salt
6 cups rice cereal
1 cup crushed chocolate sandwich cookies

Pretty much everyone I know has a fond childhood memory of crispy, gooey cereal treats. When I was really little, my family used to make a big batch of them together almost every weekend . . . but not quite as big as this. Based on their size alone, it's easy to assume that these titanic treats came straight from the Pym Test Kitchen, but stop and think about it for a moment. If they enlarged a regular cereal treat using Pym Particles, everything would increase proportionally, right? That would mean grains of puffed rice the size of your fist (which would probably not be very much fun to eat). So how did we get them to be so big then? I'm not legally allowed to speak about that technology publicly yet. But let's just say that our neighbors on the Avengers Campus aren't the only ones exploring innovative ways to increase the food supply through science. Some people say competition breeds excellence . . . I say it breeds deliciousness!

INSTRUCTIONS

1. Prep an 8-by-8-inch pan with parchment sprayed with nonstick spray. Set aside.
2. In a large Dutch oven, melt butter over low heat. Add the marshmallows. Let melt for 2 to 3 minutes, then stir until combined. Stir in the vanilla and salt.
3. Remove from heat, then fold in the rice cereal and crushed cookies until completely coated.
4. Press into the prepped pan and let cool.

PYM

YIELD: 12 SERVINGS DIFFICULTY: DIFFICULT

SPIDER-BOT CUPCAKES

PREP TIME: 1 HOUR > COOK TIME: 15 MIN

Hey there! Peter Parker here. I was the lead engineer on the Slinger Project at the Worldwide Engineering Brigade. Working alongside Cassie and the rest of our amazing team of innovators was something I'll always remember, though there were a few key moments that I might try to forget. On the top of that list is the time when our Spider-Bots—the robotic helpers we designed to break down raw material and create all kinds of useful tech—got stuck in self-replication mode and started multiplying at an alarming rate, consuming everything in their path. That was not the best way to start the Worldwide Engineering Brigade open house. ~~If I hadn't~~ If Spider-Man hadn't shown up when he did, it could've led to the devastation of the entire Avengers Campus! On the bright side, these spectacular Spider-Bot cupcakes that my Aunt May baked for us (before everything went haywire) were just about the only things the little guys didn't consume. If you ask me, they totally missed out!

CUPCAKES:

2 cups all-purpose flour
1/2 cup cocoa powder
1/2 teaspoon baking powder
1/4 teaspoon kosher salt
1/2 cup (1 stick) unsalted softened butter
1 cup granulated sugar
1/2 cup light brown sugar
2 large eggs
1 teaspoon vanilla extract
1 cup chocolate milk

FROSTING:

1 cup (2 sticks) unsalted butter, softened
1 teaspoon vanilla extract
1/4 teaspoon kosher salt
5 cups confectioners' sugar
2 to 3 tablespoons whole milk
Red food gel dye, as needed

DECORATION:

32 pieces red licorice, cut into thirds
6 pieces blue taffy, rolled out and halved
24 blue candy-coated chocolates

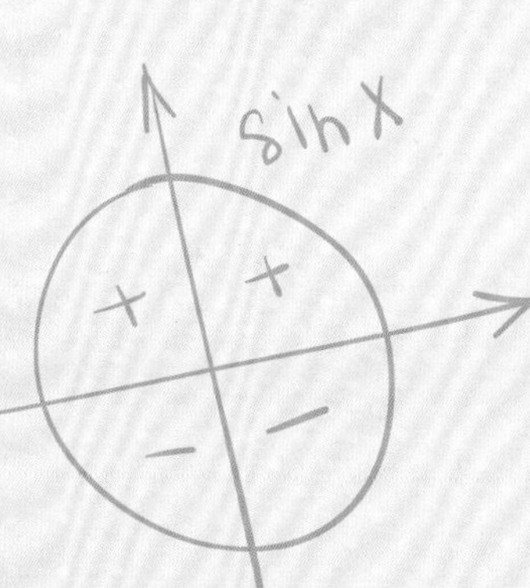

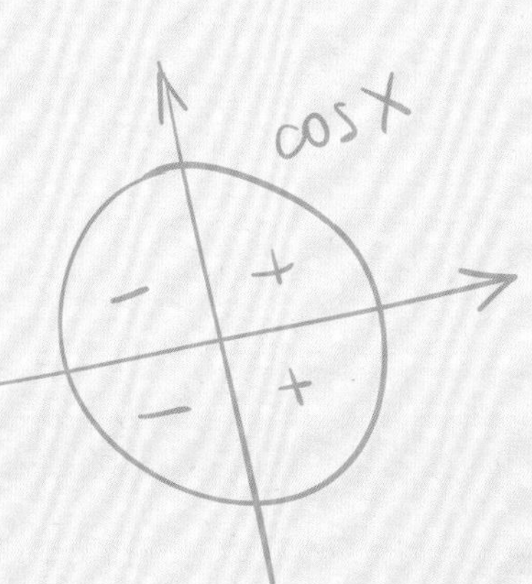

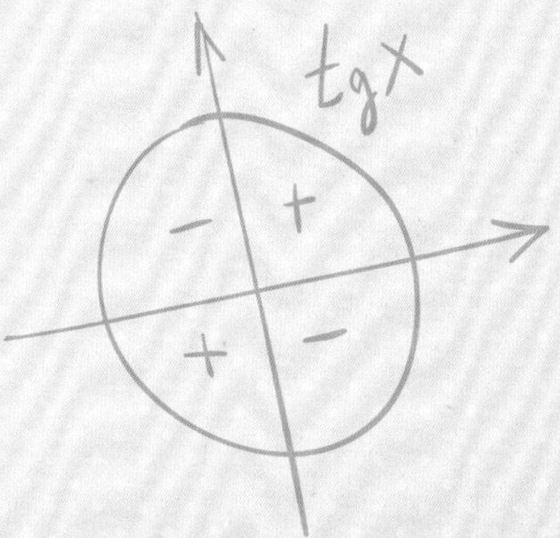

RECIPE CONTINUES ON NEXT PAGE...

INSTRUCTIONS >>>>>>>

Make the cupcakes:

1. Preheat the oven to 350°F. Prep a cupcake pan with liners.
2. In a medium bowl, whisk together the flour, cocoa powder, baking powder, and salt. Set aside.
3. In the bowl of an electric mixer, cream the butter, sugar, and brown sugar until fluffy.
4. Add the eggs and vanilla, mixing until just combined.
5. Alternate adding the dry ingredients and the chocolate milk, mixing until just combined.
6. Fill liners $^2/_3$ full and bake for 15 to 17 minutes until cooked through. Let cool on a wire rack.

Make the frosting:

7. In the bowl of an electric mixer, stir together the butter, vanilla, and salt. Add the confectioners' sugar, milk, and red food gel dye, mixing to a piping consistency.

To decorate:

8. Pipe the red frosting onto the cooled cupcakes. Place the blue taffy on the tops of the heads, then add the blue candy-coated chocolate to create the eyes.
9. Take the licorice pieces and press four into each side of each cupcake for a total of eight legs.
10. Once the cupcakes have been decorated, they're ready to serve.

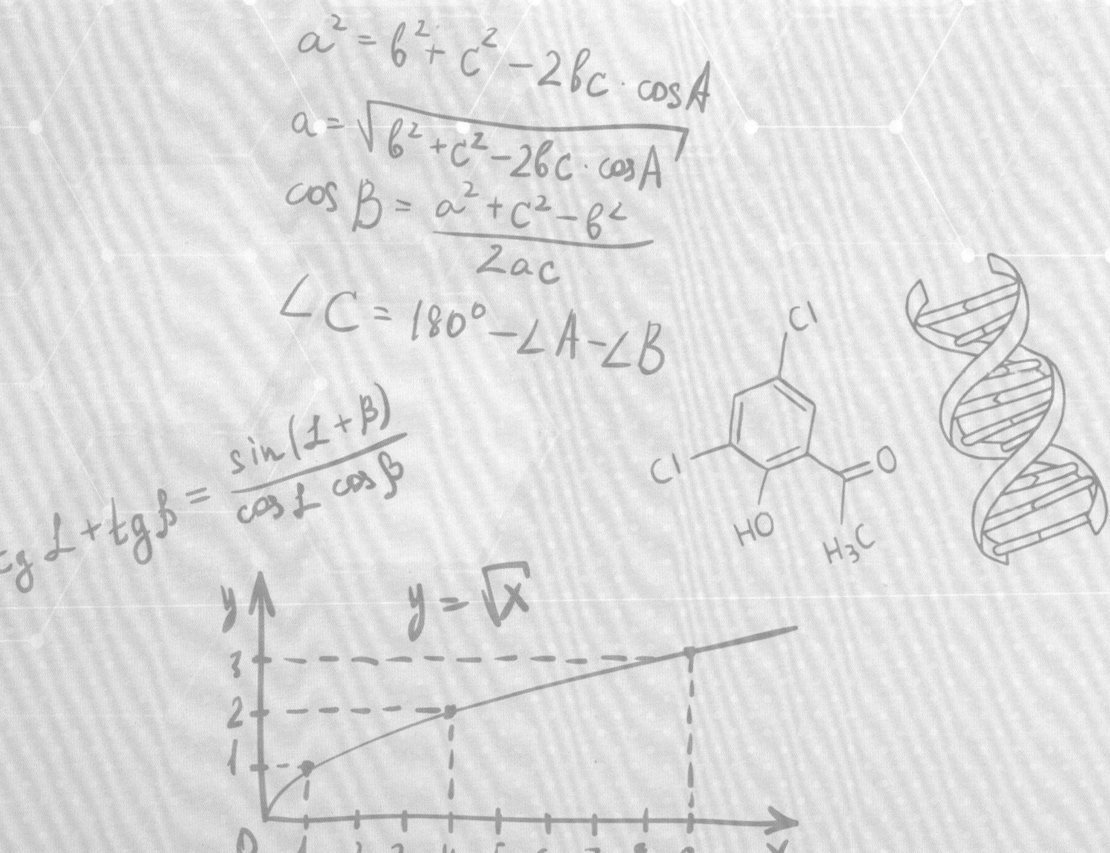

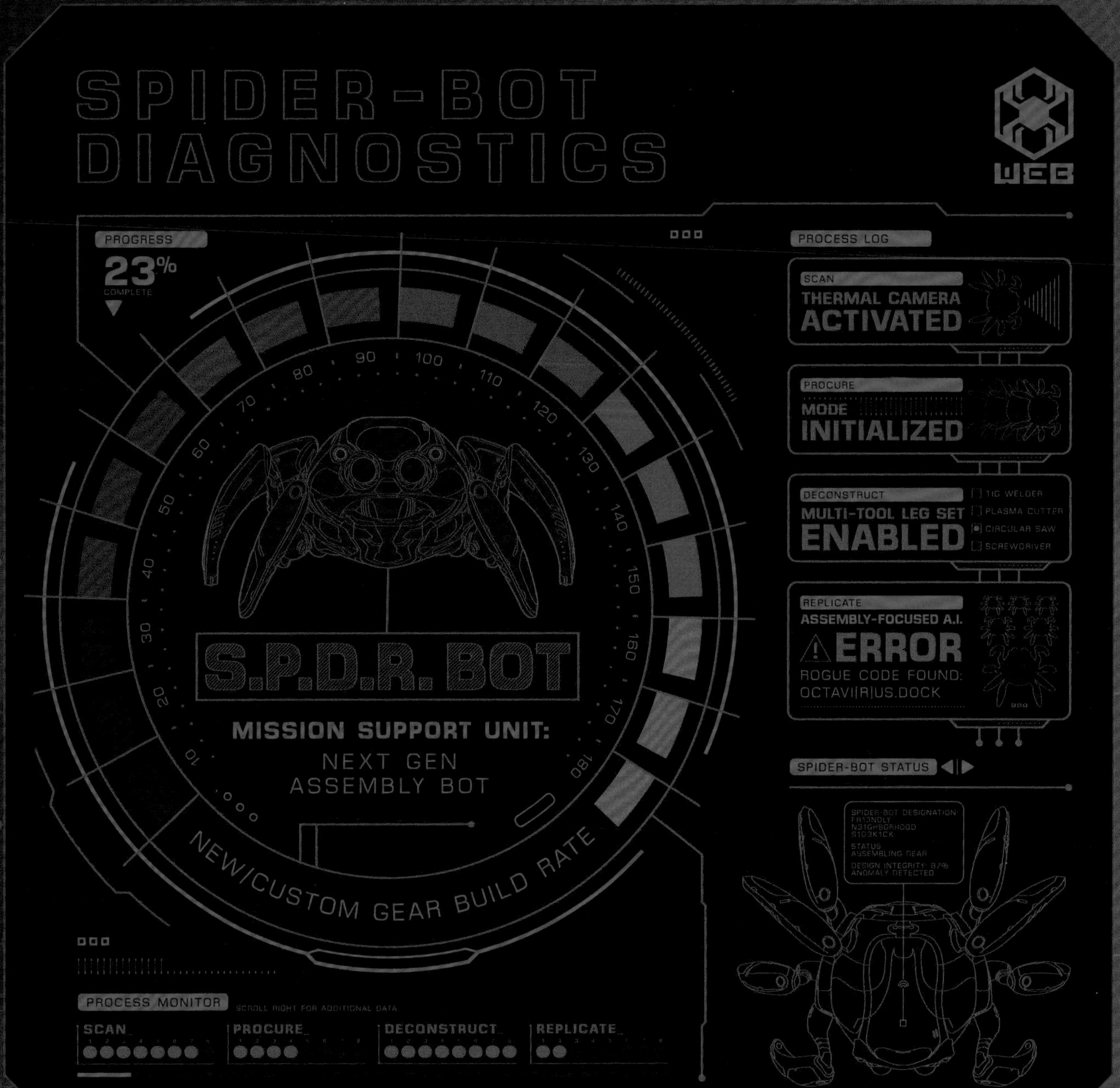

SPIDER-BOT DIAGNOSTICS

PROGRESS

23%
COMPLETE

S.P.D.R. BOT

MISSION SUPPORT UNIT:

NEXT GEN
ASSEMBLY BOT

NEW/CUSTOM GEAR BUILD RATE

PROCESS LOG

SCAN
THERMAL CAMERA
ACTIVATED

PROCURE
MODE
INITIALIZED

DECONSTRUCT
MULTI-TOOL LEG SET
ENABLED

- TIG WELDER
- PLASMA CUTTER
- CIRCULAR SAW
- SCREWDRIVER

REPLICATE
ASSEMBLY-FOCUSED A.I.
⚠ERROR
ROGUE CODE FOUND:
OCTAVI|R|US.DOCK

SPIDER-BOT STATUS

SPIDER-BOT DESIGNATION
FR13NDLY
N31GHBORHOOD
S103K1CK

STATUS
ASSEMBLING GEAR

DESIGN INTEGRITY: 87%
ANOMALY DETECTED

PROCESS MONITOR
SCROLL RIGHT FOR ADDITIONAL DATA

SCAN_ | PROCURE_ | DECONSTRUCT_ | REPLICATE_

YIELD: 8 SERVINGS   DIFFICULTY: MEDIUM

GOLIATH-SIZE COOKIES

PREP TIME: 20 MIN > COOK TIME: 20 MIN

- 2 cups all-purpose flour
- 1 cup oats
- 1 teaspoon baking soda
- 1/2 teaspoon kosher salt
- 1/2 cup (1 stick) unsalted butter, softened
- 1 cup peanut butter
- 1 cup packed light brown sugar
- 3/4 cup granulated sugar
- 2 teaspoons vanilla extract
- 2 large eggs
- 1 cup chocolate chips
- 1 cup candy-coated chocolates
- 1 cup mini pretzels

When my dad puts on his super hero gear, he becomes the astonishing Ant-Man—which is a really great code name for a guy who shrinks down to the size of a bug. But it kinda ignores the fact that he can also use Pym Particles to grow all huge. When he's towering over the city, the name "Ant-Man" stops making sense. We were workshopping a bunch of alternate names together and landed on a few favorites. Dad wanted to keep it simple and go with "Giant-Man," but I thought that "Goliath" had more flare to it. "Goliath" just makes you think of something enormous, right? Like, something so that big it's almost intimidating. Just to sell the point, I had the Pym Test Kitchen whip up a batch of these Goliath-Sized Cookies, chock-full of chocolate chips, candy pieces, peanut butter, and pretzel bits. When it comes to the name, I'm still not sure if Dad's going to bite . . . but when it comes to the cookies, he had no problem whatsoever!

INSTRUCTIONS

1. Preheat the oven to 350°F and line baking sheets with silicone baking mat.
2. In a large bowl, whisk together the flour, oats, baking soda, and salt. Set aside.
3. In the bowl of an electric mixer, cream the butter, peanut butter, brown sugar, and granulated sugar. Add the vanilla and the eggs until combined.
4. Spoon in the dry ingredients and keep mixing until the dough comes together.
5. Fold in the chocolate chips, candy-coated chocolates, and pretzels.
6. Form the dough into 8 large balls. Place on the prepped sheets and flatten.
7. Bake for 20 minutes until browned and cooked through. Let cool on a wire rack.

NOTE TO SELF: "STATURE" ALSO SOUNDS SUPERCOOL. HANG ON TO THAT ONE . . .
-CASSIE

YIELD: 4 SERVINGS   DIFFICULTY: MEDIUM

WEB FRITTERS

PREP TIME: 10 MIN > COOK TIME: 3 MIN

Peter Parker is the Worldwide Engineering Brigade's resident expert in high-tensile synthetics and fluid dynamics. He used that brilliant brain of his to create a multiuser delivery device for synthetic webbing (basically reverse engineering Spider-Man's Web-Shooters). Once Pete perfected his basic design, the rest of us here at the Worldwide Engineering Brigade started to tinker with our own versions, adding all sorts of cool extra effects into the mix. You should see all the wild ideas we came up with (and maybe someday soon you will)! One of my favorite modifications ditched the super-sticky adhesive fluid altogether and replaced it with a sweet edible compound similar to the batter used for making funnel cakes at a fair. When propelled through the Web-Shooter, the batter comes out in an arachnid-approved arrangement that makes it look as if Spidey himself was manning the deep fryer! (If you don't have a Web-Shooter handy, you can always pour it in a web-shaped pattern yourself.) This web isn't great for eliminating rogue Spider-Bots, but it does a heck of a job when it comes to defeating my appetite!

4 cups vegetable oil, for frying
1½ cups pancake mix
1 teaspoon pumpkin pie spice
¼ teaspoon kosher salt
¾ cup whole milk
1 teaspoon vanilla extract

ICING:
1 cup confectioners' sugar
2 tablespoons whole milk
1 tablespoon unsalted butter, softened

SPECIAL SUPPLIES:
Funnel or pastry bag

INSTRUCTIONS

1. In a Dutch oven, heat oil to 350°F.
2. In a large bowl, whisk together pancake mix, pumpkin pie spice, and salt.
3. Make a well in the center of the dry ingredients and stir in the milk and vanilla until the batter is thin and pourable.
4. Use a funnel or pastry bag to swirl ¼ of the batter, making a web shape in the hot oil.
5. Cook for 1 minute, then flip over and cook for another 1 to 2 minutes until golden brown. Let drain on a wire rack. Repeat with the remaining batter.
6. In a small bowl, whisk together the confectioners' sugar, milk, and butter until smooth. Drizzle the icing onto each funnel cake and serve.

Make sure to mark this Web-Shooter clearly so Spidey doesn't end up shooting raw batter at his enemies (again)!
-Peter

PYM
TECHNOLOGIES

CHAPTER 5

FROM THE PYM TASTING LAB

BEVERAGES

According to a meme I once saw, Thomas Edison (who was like, one of the greatest inventors who ever lived) said, "Genius is 1 percent inspiration and 99 percent perspiration." After spending a long, hot summer on the Avengers Campus trying to come up with groundbreaking new ideas, I can now confirm his statement to be 100 percent true. But despite how desperately we at Worldwide Engineering Brigade required regular rehydration, our team had one simple rule: "Don't drink what's in the beaker, no matter how delicious it looks!" Sure, there was a decent chance that Onome was just boiling up some hibiscus tea, but it was also equally likely that Peter was concocting an enhanced version of that super-sticky adhesive fluid of his. With most liquids off-limits, we were all thrilled when the Pym Test Kitchen expanded its operations to include a beverage-focused branch known as the Pym Tasting Lab. While their major focus has been on innovative brewing techniques for adult beverages, they were willing to collaborate with us to concoct this list of libations appropriate for all ages. While these fluid formulations are equally as experimental, at least it's guaranteed that they're safe to consume. And after a long, hot day of changing the world, there's nothing more refreshing than a tall, cold glass of science!

YIELD: 1 SERVING DIFFICULTY: EASY

SMASH SLUSH

PREP TIME: 5 MIN, PLUS AN ADDITIONAL 24 HOURS FOR FREEZING > COOK TIME: N/A

1 cup orange-pineapple soda
1/2 cup lemon-lime soda
1/4 teaspoon clear vanilla extract
1/2 cup vanilla ice cream

There's this imported Brazilian soda called Pingo Doce that's become all the rage around the Avengers Campus since the Pym Test Kitchen started offering it through their soda fountain. According to its marketing material, Pingo Doce (which translates to "sweet drop" in Portuguese) "RADIATES delicious flavor to SMASH your thirst!" Apparently, there's more truth to that than anyone would like to admit. A little digging on the web revealed that a bottle of this stuff became contaminated with gamma radiation a few years back! It sounds like it was just a freak accident, so I'm not that worried, but I still limit my intake for other reasons. The original recipe uses guarana, a native Amazonian plant with a bit too much caffeine for me. (I'm a teenager. I already have enough energy, thanks.) Luckily, we've managed to formulate a slushy substitute that captures Pingo Doce's fabulous flavor—though we couldn't quite capture its glorious gamma-green color—without keeping me awake for hours on end!

INSTRUCTIONS >>>>>

1. Pour orange-pineapple soda into an ice cube tray and place in the freezer overnight.
2. Add the frozen soda cubes into the base of a blender. Pour in the lemon-lime soda and vanilla and blend until slushy.
3. Pour into a tall glass and top with vanilla ice cream.

V GF

YIELD: 1 SERVING DIFFICULTY: EASY

PROTON PB&J PUNCH

PREP TIME: 5 MIN > COOK TIME: N/A

Before the Pym Test Kitchen starts serving its experimental eats to the public, they perform a rigorous R&D process behind closed kitchen doors. There are hundreds of alternate options for each dish that are developed and discarded before a final version makes it onto the menu for your tasting and testing. On a rare occasion, two divergent dishes with the same point of origin make it across the finish line for public trials. You remember the PB3 Superb Sandwich (page 45), right? Well, it turns out another variation of those classic flavors evolved during the early exploratory phase, this one in drinkable form. The Proton PB&J Punch is sort of like lemonade, but with notes of peanut butter and strawberry. If you've ever wanted to sip a sandwich through a straw, this is the supersweet solution!

LEMONADE:

$1\frac{1}{2}$ cups lemonade

2 tablespoons strawberry syrup

1 tablespoon peanut butter syrup

TOPPING:

$\frac{1}{2}$ cup heavy whipping cream

2 teaspoons peanut butter syrup

3 to 4 mini peanut butter cookies

INSTRUCTIONS >>>>>>

1. In a small pitcher, whisk lemonade, strawberry syrup, and peanut butter syrup. Keep in the refrigerator until ready to serve.
2. In a small bowl, use a hand mixer to whip the heavy cream and peanut butter syrup until soft peaks form. Set aside.
3. Pour the lemonade mix over ice into a tall glass. Top with the peanut butter whipped cream and the peanut butter cookies.

ONOME'S
OUTREACH

PYM
TECHNOLOGIES
SPECTRAL-COLOR
COLA
PYM
TECHNOLOGIES
FRUIT
FRACTION
STARK'S SYNERGY SLUSH

PYM
TECHNOLOGIES

YIELD: 4 SERVINGS | DIFFICULTY: EASY

FRUIT FRACTION

PREP TIME: 10 MIN > COOK TIME: N/A

SIMPLE SYRUP:

1/2 cup water

1/2 cup granulated sugar

PUNCH:

12 ounces mango nectar

1/2 cup lime juice

1 1/2 cups water

1 lime cut into rounds, for garnish

Scientific experimentation isn't always as exciting as they make it look in the movies. You know how they're always mixing together a bunch of volatile chemicals until they erupt in a wild chemical reaction? That's so not what we do at the Worldwide Engineering Brigade. (Okay, maybe it's what Peter does, but that's usually by accident.) Most days, we're simply running the same trials over and over, making the slightest adjustments to our formulae as we go until we find the one that works. It may not always be thrilling, but the results are undeniably rewarding. This refreshing drink is one of those results—a punch made from mango nectar, lime juice, and simple syrup. The main ingredients were pretty much the same from the start, but we spent three days in the Pym Tasting Lab tweaking the ratios down to a fraction of a milliliter. What we ended up with is a faultless fusion of fruity flavors that explodes with tropical taste (without any worries that it'll explode in your face)!

INSTRUCTIONS

Make the simple syrup:

1. In a small saucepan, bring the water and sugar to a boil, stirring until the sugar has dissolved, and liquid is clear. Let cool completely.

Make the punch:

2. In a small pitcher, stir together the mango nectar, lime juice, and water. Stir in the simple syrup.
3. Pour over ice and add lime rounds to serve.

Hey! It was one explosion! Wait . . . two. Two explosions! (Definitely no more than three . . .)
–Peter

V

V+

GF

YIELD: 4 SERVINGS DIFFICULTY: EASY

GINGER BUZZ

PREP TIME: 3 HOURS > COOK TIME: 10 MIN

4 cups water
1 cup honey
Two 2-inch slices ginger
3/4 cup lemon juice
1/2 cup sweetened condensed milk

My dad isn't just called Ant-Man because he can shrink down to itty-bitty bug size. He also has a piece of state-of-the-art Pym Tech built into his helmet that allows him to communicate with insects by using electromagnetic pulses to mimic their pheromones. You'd think he'd use it to do some pretty astonishing things, but mostly he just tries to get groups of ants to perform choreography from '90s boy band videos together. (I worry about him sometimes.) On the plus side, Hope has the same EMP Communication Device integrated into her own helmet. And while she may be known as the Wasp, she managed to negotiate a fair-trade deal with a local colony of honeybees, providing the Pym Test Kitchen with a nearly unlimited supply of fresh honey for use in their recipes. One of my favorite creations to come out of that collaboration is this creamy honey-ginger lemonade. This is the drink that everyone around the Avengers Campus has been buzzing about!

INSTRUCTIONS

1. In a large saucepan, bring water, honey, and ginger to a boil. Turn off heat and let cool. Remove the ginger and place the simple syrup in water (uncovered) in the refrigerator for 2 to 3 hours or until cold.
2. In a large pitcher, stir together the simple syrup and lemon juice. Whisk in the sweetened condensed milk. Pour over ice to serve.

V GF

YIELD: 1 SERVING — DIFFICULTY: EASY

NEURO-FREEZE

PREP TIME: 10 MIN > COOK TIME: N/A

TOPPING:

2 ounces mascarpone, softened

2 tablespoons confectioners' sugar

1/4 cup heavy whipping cream

FREEZE:

2 cups vanilla ice cream

One 12-oz can root beer

Sphenopa-what? My brain froze just trying to figure out how to pronounce that! –Dad

This summer, almost everyone on the Avengers Campus found themselves suffering from an occasional case of *sphenopalatine ganglioneuralgia*. Oh, don't worry . . . that's not some weird flesh-eating virus created by A.I.M. or anything. It's just the fancy scientific term for what most people call "brain freeze"—that quick but painful little headache that you get when you drink something really, really cold really, really fast. One of the main culprits was this amazing, blended combo of root beer and vanilla ice cream the Pym Tasting Lab whipped up for us. It's icy cold, super creamy, and has just the right amount of bite. During the initial testing phase, we at the Worldwide Engineering Brigade had a contest to see how fast we could chug these down . . . and, well, now you know how this one got its name! If you make one for yourself, I suggest drinking it at a regular pace so that you can really savor the flavors (and avoid any nasty side effects).

INSTRUCTIONS

1. In a small bowl, stir together the mascarpone and confectioners' sugar. Add heavy whipping cream and whisk until light and fluffy, 1 to 2 minutes. Keep in the refrigerator to chill.
2. In the base of a blender, add the vanilla ice cream and root beer. Blend until smooth.
3. Pour into a glass and top with whipped mascarpone to serve.

V GF

YIELD: 1 SERVING

DIFFICULTY: EASY

SPECTRAL-COLOR COLA

PREP TIME: 5 MIN > COOK TIME: N/A

2 tablespoons maraschino cherry juice
1 tablespoon grenadine
1 tablespoon lime juice
1 cup ice
10 ounces cola, chilled
1 lime wedge, for serving
1 maraschino cherry, for serving

Some historians (and probably most of the staff on the Avengers Campus) seem to support the notion that science is fueled by coffee. But when you bring a bunch of teenagers like us into the lab, you have to switch things over to an alternative energy source—an endless stream of soda! True story: The Worldwide Engineering Brigade went through so many cases of cola that the team at the Pym Test Kitchen finally decided to supersize—and ceiling-mount—a bunch of soda cans to supply their fountain machine. (The process also enlarged the bubbles . . . and the burps!) Then the soda scientists from the Pym Tasting Lab figured out how to mix and match flavors with the touch of a screen, allowing us to craft endless carbonated combos. This is one of my signature creations, a classic cola with a sweet, syrupy cherry layer at the bottom. In the light of our lab, it gets this ghostly glow that makes it look even cooler than it tastes. A few glasses of this bubbly beverage really get the science flowing!

INSTRUCTIONS

1. In a tall glass, combine the maraschino cherry juice, grenadine, and lime juice. Add the ice, then the cola.
2. Serve with the lime wedge and cherry.

V V+ GF

YIELD: 1 SERVING | DIFFICULTY: EASY

A STUDY IN MARSHMALLOWS

PREP TIME: 10 MIN > COOK TIME: N/A

SHAKE:

1 cup mini marshmallows
2 cups vanilla ice cream
1/2 cup whole milk
1 teaspoon clear vanilla extract
1/4 teaspoon kosher salt

TOPPING:

1/4 cup marshmallow crème
1/4 cup whipped cream
3 regular marshmallows

SPECIAL SUPPLIES:

Kitchen torch

Fun food fact: Did you know that marshmallows are equal parts solid and gas? Hard to believe, I know, but approximately 50% of every sweet, chewy little blob of sugar is nothing more than air. Their teeny tiny internal bubbles are equalized with the external atmospheric pressure, helping marshmallows keep their shape until some outside force like heat is applied. (Put one in your cosmic-powered convection oven and you'll see what I mean!) While I appreciate the equilibrium, the Pym Tasting Lab is all about shaking things up—or in this case, milkshaking things up! They took a food that is delicately balanced between two states of matter and transformed it into another state altogether—liquid. That's right, this creamy milkshake tastes like a marshmallow in drinkable form! For those who still crave the sponginess of this semi-solid sweet, a topping of torch-toasted marshies is included in an effort to properly represent all three states of scrumptiousness!

INSTRUCTIONS

1. Place the mini marshmallows on a foil-lined baking sheet and use a kitchen torch to brown. Add to the base of a blender along with the vanilla ice cream, whole milk, clear vanilla, and salt. Blend until just combined.
2. Roll the rim of a tall glass in marshmallow crème. Pour in the milkshake and top with whipped cream.
3. Place the marshmallows on top and use the kitchen torch to brown. Serve immediately.

YIELD: 1 SERVING

DIFFICULTY: MEDIUM

ONOME'S OUTREACH

PREP TIME: 5 MIN > COOK TIME: N/A

3/4 cup coconut milk
1/4 cup blackberries, smashed
1 tablespoon granulated sugar
1/4 teaspoon clear vanilla extract
1/3 cup whipped coconut cream, for garnish
3 to 5 blackberries, for garnish

The African nation of Wakanda has been one of the world's best-kept secrets for centuries, shielding its unparalleled technological advancements from the prying eyes of those who live beyond their borders. But in recent years, thanks to the efforts of King T'Challa and his sister Shuri, Wakanda has begun to share both its rich history and its keen focus on the future with the rest of the world. Their Wakandan Outreach program even sent a delegate to join the Worldwide Engineering Brigade. Our girl Onome fit right in here at the Worldwide Engineering Brigade from moment one, teaching us all kinds of cool new things, from how to say "hello" in Xhosa ("Mholo!") to how to program Kimoyo beads. She also shared some awesome recipes from her culture, like this traditional chilled beverage made with blackberry-infused coconut milk. She says its purple hue proudly invokes Wakanda's greatest resource—Vibranium. The only way this drink could be better is if it gave us cool panther powers!

INSTRUCTIONS

1. In a small saucepan over medium heat, simmer the coconut milk, blackberries, sugar, and vanilla until the sugar has dissolved, 3 to 5 minutes. Let cool.
2. Fill a glass with ice, then pour in the coconut milk mixture. Top with whipped cream and whole blackberries to serve.

I'M AFRAID SOME RECIPES ARE RESERVED FOR WAKANDA'S RULER ALONE . . . -ONOME

V V+ GF

YIELD: 1 SERVING

DIFFICULTY: EASY

STARK'S SYNERGY SLUSH

PREP TIME: 5 MIN, ADDITIONAL 8 HOURS FOR FREEZING > COOKTIME: N/A

- 1½ cups fruit punch, divided
- 1 cup frozen peaches
- ½ cup orange juice
- 1 tablespoon lemon juice

I don't think I'm breaking any headlines when I say that there are few things Tony Stark loves more than himself. His heightened level of self-admiration carries over into all his business ventures—including the Worldwide Engineering Brigade. If there's enough room to slap a Stark Industries logo onto one of our innovations, you can bet he will. It's a level of corporate synergy unlike anything I've ever seen. Heck, even the slushie machine that he had installed in the Worldwide Engineering Brigade Workshop break room is only authorized to serve its fruity frozen drinks in signature Iron Man red and gold—not that we're complaining, of course. Both the golden peach and red fruit punch slushes are top-notch on their own—and they're even better when layered together! Who knows, maybe someday when I'm a genius billionaire philanthropist, I'll get a drink designed after me. And if I do, I hope it's this good!

INSTRUCTIONS >>>>>

1. Pour 1 cup of the fruit punch into an ice cube tray. Freeze for 8 hours or until solid.
2. Place the frozen fruit punch cubes into the base of a blender along with the remaining ½ cup. Blend until slushy and pour into a tall glass.
3. Rinse out the blender and add the frozen peaches, orange juice, and lemon juice. Blend until slushy. Pour on top of the fruit punch slush to serve.

BEVERAGES

V

V+

GF

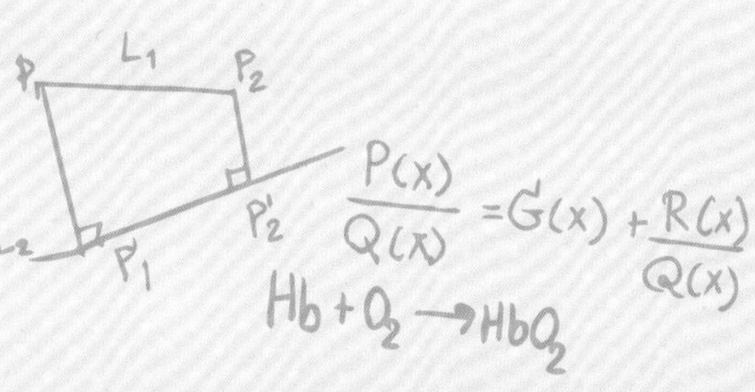

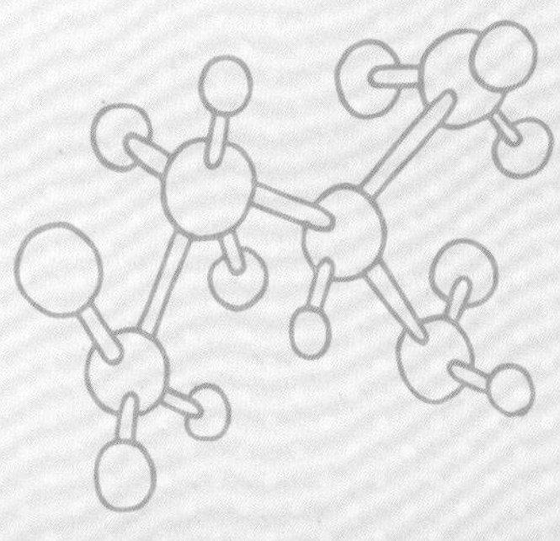

YIELD: 1 SERVING DIFFICULTY: MEDIUM

THYME VARIANT TEA

PREP TIME: 15 MIN > COOK TIME: 10 MIN

- 2 cups water
- 1 tablespoon honey
- 1 cinnamon stick
- ½ medium Granny Smith apple, cored and sliced (reserve 2 slices for garnish)
- 1 green tea bag
- 2 sprigs fresh thyme (reserve 1 sprig for garnish)

Thor and his fellow Asgardians love to throw epic feasts where "the mead flows like a river!" For those of us who aren't quite old enough to imbibe the nectar of the gods, however, there are usually plenty of other options available to wash down all that boar and Bilgesnipe (which, surprisingly, tastes a lot like chicken). One of them is a fruity herbal tea that gets its flavor from the legendary Golden Apples of Idunn—the same apples that give Asgardians their immortality! It's so heavenly that we asked the Pym Tasting Lab to help us figure out how to brew some ourselves. Since the odds of getting our hands on any of Asgard's most sacred apples were less than zero, they came up with this copycat formula that uses regular green apples and thyme. It tastes almost exactly the same, but with enough subtle differences to keep things interesting. Unless you've got a hookup from the God of Mischief himself, this low-key variant is the best you'll get.

INSTRUCTIONS

1. In a medium saucepan over medium heat, bring the water, honey, cinnamon stick, and apple slices (reserving 2 for garnish) to a boil. Reduce heat to low and simmer for 2 minutes.
2. Add the tea bag and 1 sprig thyme and let steep for 10 minutes. Strain into a pitcher, let cool for 10 minutes, then refrigerate until chilled.
3. To serve, pour over ice and garnish with apple slices and remaining thyme.

V GF

YIELD: 4 SERVINGS   DIFFICULTY: EASY

PHOTON POWER PUNCH

PREP TIME: 10 MIN > COOK TIME: N/A

SIMPLE SYRUP:

1/2 cup water

1/2 cup granulated sugar

PUNCH:

6 ounces pineapple juice

1/2 cup lemon juice

1 1/2 cups cold sparkling water

1 pint pineapple sorbet

Hope van Dyne may be the boss of Pym Technologies, but Carol Danvers—aka Captain Marvel—is the undisputed boss of space. She's one of the most powerful heroes to ever soar through the stars, saving entire galaxies without a single hair ever falling out of place. It's kinda insane. But also amazing. When we heard Captain Marvel was coming to the Avengers Campus for a visit, I fangirled out and practically begged the Pym Tasting Lab to come up with a special signature drink in her honor. Distilling her heroic essence down to liquid form might seem like a tall order, but my favorite mixological masterminds came through once again, concocting this tart pineapple lemonade enhanced by a scoop of cool pineapple sorbet. Glowing as brightly as the Captain does in her Binary form and packing a punch strong enough to knock Thanos on his ugly purple behind, this drink is a truly a marvel!

INSTRUCTIONS

Make the simple syrup:

1. In a small saucepan, bring the water and sugar to a boil, stirring until liquid is clear and the sugar has dissolved. Let cool completely.

Make the punch:

2. In a small pitcher, pour in the pineapple juice, lemon juice, and sparkling water. Stir in the simple syrup.
3. To serve, pour over ice and add a scoop of pineapple sorbet on top.

GF V+ V

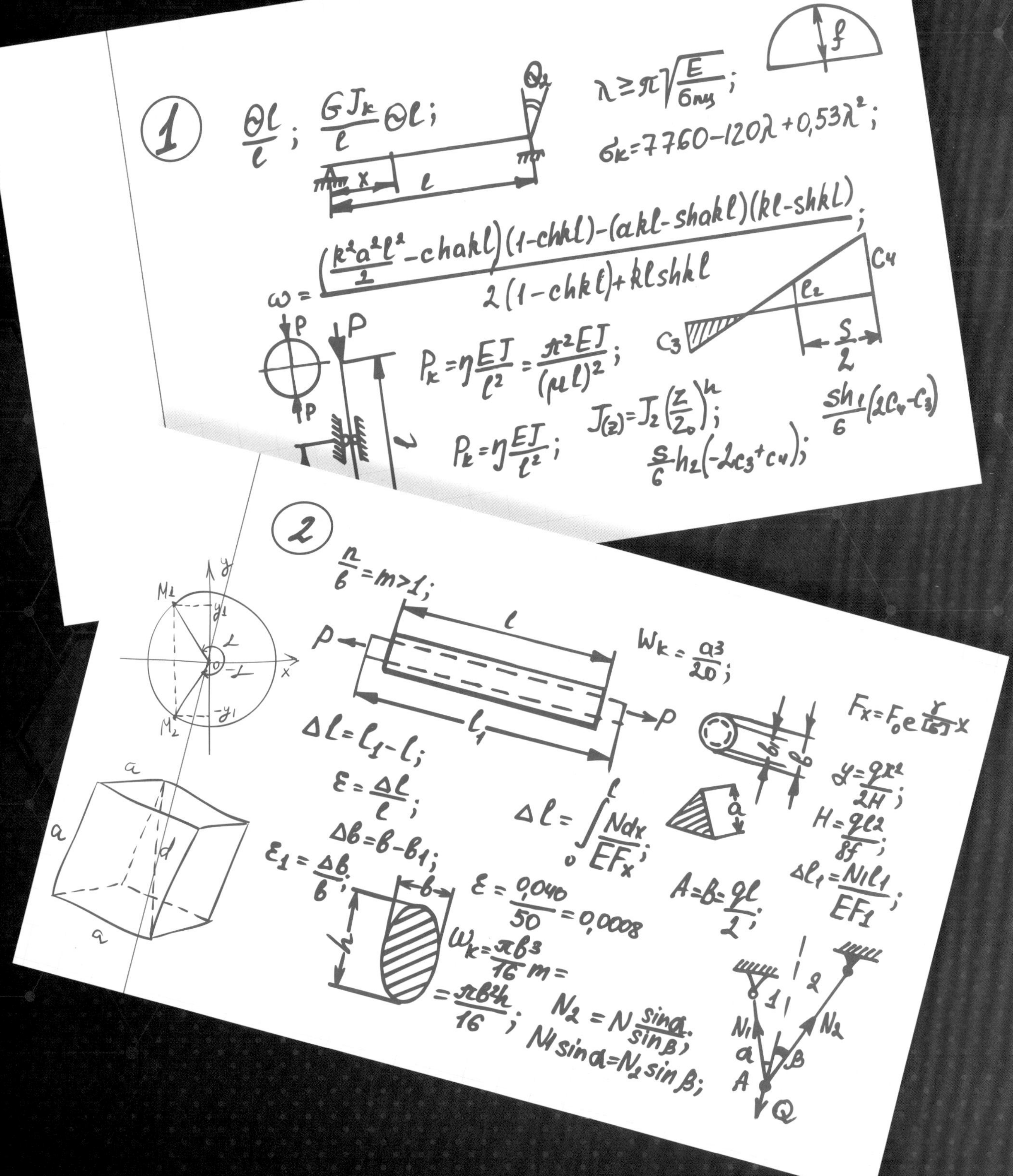

1
σк=7760−120λ+0,53λ²;
2
n/b=m>1;
Wк = a³/20;
Δl=l1−l;
ε = Δl/l;
Δb=b−b1;
ε1 = Δb/b;
ε = 0,040/50 = 0,0008
A=B=ql/2;
N2 = N sinα/sinβ;
N1 sinα=N2 sinβ;

YIELD: 1 SERVING

DIFFICULTY: EASY

WEB SLINGER

PREP TIME: 10 MIN > COOK TIME: N/A

GARNISH:

1 strawberry
Chocolate icing
White icing

DRINK:

1 cup ice
1 cup fruit punch
1 cup zero sugar blue sports drink

We may have all come from different regions of the world and had totally unique areas of expertise, but over the course of our time on the Avengers Campus, the young innovators at the Worldwide Engineering Brigade (WEB) became more than just a team; we became a family. We celebrated each member's successes as if they were our own and helped each other recover from our failures (trust me, there were plenty). Whenever my fellow WEB-heads want to visit me back at home, my doors will always be open. And if they all decide to come at the same time . . . well, hopefully we have enough Pym Particles on hand to fit everyone comfortably into the house! I may be headed back to the Bay Area now, but every time I pour myself a WEB Slinger—this sweet, fruity beverage proudly layered in our team's signature red and blue—I'll be thinking about everything we accomplished. We might not be heroes (at least not yet!), but I'd like to think we made the world a better place together . . . maybe just a little.

INSTRUCTIONS

1. Use the chocolate icing to pipe the webbing onto the strawberry. Pipe eyes using the white icing. Set aside.
2. Add ice to a large glass. Pour in the fruit punch. Top with the blue sports drink. Add the strawberry garnish to the glass to serve.

V GF

Love you, Cassie!
-Doreen
WEB
SUPPLIERS

You're my hero!
-Lunella

Keep in touch!
-Harley

Safe journeys, my friend!
-Onome

So proud of you, Bug!
-Dad

Call me next time you're in Queens!
-Peter

DIETARY CONSIDERATIONS CHART

- **V** = Vegetarian
- **V+** = Vegan
- **GF** = Gluten-free

SIZED TO SHARE (APPETIZERS)

Quantum Pretzel with Cheese Sauce **V**

Cosmic Krackle Corn **V, GF**

Ants on a Log **V, GF**

Golden Wakanda Wedges **V, GF**

Snack Molecules **V**

Eggs-Periment 2.0 **V, GF**

Rice-Osceles Triangles **V, V+, GF**

Bacon Analysis **GF**

BIG BITES (MAIN DISHES)

Pepper Potts's Arc Reactor Discs **V, GF**

Impossible™ Spoonful **V, V+**

Impossible™ Victory Falafel Shawarma **V, V+**

Soup and Sandwich Symmetry **V**

INDEPENDENT VARIABLES (SIDE DISHES)

Galactic Greens **V, GF**

Caesar Salad + Colossal Crouton **V**

Cosmic Cheese Fusion **V, GF**

Kinetic Cauliflower **V, V+, GF**

Doctor Strange's Bubbling Cauldron **GF**

Bifrost Fruit Salad **V, GF**

Formidable Frites **V, GF**

Macroscopic Mac & Cheese **V**

Quantum Entangled Noodle Salad **V, V+**

Wasp's Stinging Corn Cobs **V, GF**

CONFECTIONARY CONCLUSIONS (DESSERTS)

Peach Pym Pies **V**

Celestial-size Choco-Smash Sundae **V**

Transcendental Terran Spirals **V**

Multiversal Multilayered Frozen Orb **V, GF**

Lunella's Moon Pies **V**

Doreen's Nutty Brownies **V**

Molecular Mochi Munchies **V, GF**

Mega Cereal Treats **V**

Spider-Bot Cupcakes **V**

Goliath-Size Cookies **V**

WEB Fritters **V**

FROM THE PYM TASTING LAB (BEVERAGES)

Smash Slush **V, GF**

Proton PB&J Punch **V**

Fruit Fraction **V, V+, GF**

Ginger Buzz **V, GF**

Neuro-Freeze **V, GF**

Spectral-Color Cola **V, V+, GF**

A Study in Marshmallows **V**

Onome's Outreach **V, V+, GF**

Stark's Synergy Slush **V, V+, GF**

Thyme Variant Tea **V, GF**

Photon Power Punch **V, V+, GF**

WEB Slinger **V, GF**

Consuming raw, or undercooked eggs may increase your risk of foodborne illness.

MEASUREMENT CONVERSION CHARTS

VOLUME

CUP	OZ	TBSP	TSP	ML
1	8	16	48	240
3/4	6	12	36	180
2/3	5	11	32	160
1/2	4	8	24	120
1/3	3	5	16	80
1/4	2	4	12	60

TEMPERATURES

°F	°C
200°	93.3°
250°	120°
275°	135°
300°	150°
325°	165°
350°	177°

WEIGHT

US	METRIC
0.5 OZ	14 G
1 OZ	28 G
¼ LB	113 G
⅓ LB	151 G
½ LB	227 G
1 LB	454 G

PYM
TECHNOLOGIES

YM
T KITCHEN
Snack Molecules
T# 1710
Scott L.
TRIAL 9C
CAMPUS LAB
PYM
TECHNOLOGIES
PYM
TECHNOLOGIES

ABOUT THE AUTHORS

JENN FUJIKAWA is the lifestyle and pop culture author of *Star Wars: The Life Day Cookbook: Official Holiday Recipes From a Galaxy Far, Far Away*, *Gudetama: The Official Cookbook: Recipes for Living a Lazy Life*, *The I Love Lucy Cookbook: Classic Recipes Inspired by the Iconic TV Show*, and *The Goldbergs Cookbook*. She has created content for Disney, Ghostbusters, Lucasfilm, and more. Unique family dinners and geeky baking are a staple of her website www.justjennrecipes.com.

MARC SUMERAK is an award-winning writer who has collaborated on a number of cookbooks, including *Cooking with Deadpool*, *Star Wars: Galaxy's Edge—The Official Black Spire Outpost Cookbook*, *Star Wars: The Life Day Cookbook: Official Holiday Recipes From a Galaxy Far, Far Away*, and *The Office: The Official Party Planning Guide to Planning Parties*. Over the past two decades, his work has been featured in comics, books, and video games showcasing some of pop culture's most beloved franchises, including *Star Wars*, Ghostbusters, and many more. Find out more at www.sumerak.com. He is based in Cleveland, Ohio.

ACKNOWLEDGMENTS

FROM JENN: To the First Family, my mom Alice Kawakami, Kyle, Tyler, and Mason Fujikawa, thank you for eating so much oddly-sized food. To my brother Mark who has been on this comics-loving journey with me since birth and who I'm pretty sure has my Amazing Spider-Man Annual Vol. 1, 21. Please return it, thanks. To my very own Warriors Three who have pulled me from disaster time and time again: Mel Caylo, Chrissy Dinh, and Sarah Kuhn.

To the best taste-testers in town, the super Pool Group: Lisa Arellano, Luz Rodriguez, Caroline Sanjume, Pam Swart, and Sara Webster. To my own personal Avengers who are always ready to assemble whenever I need an assist: Troy Benjamin, Cheryl deCarvalho, Jeff Chen, Chrys Hasegawa, Liza Palmer, Robb Pearlman, Tina Pollock, and Mary Yogi. To my heroic partner Marc Sumerak—we did it! To Sammy Holland, Harrison Tunggal, and Hilary VandenBroek, thank you for steering this ship through the Quantum Realm.

One last note to my kids, please use your powers for good.

FROM MARC: To Jenn Fujikawa, my culinary companion on this epic adventure into scrumptious super-heroics. To Sammy Holland, Harrison Tunggal, and Hilary VandenBroek for helping us weave this wonderful WEB. To the amazing teams at Disney, including Brent Strong and every Imagineer who brought Avengers Campus to life. To Stan Lee, Jack Kirby, and every talented creator who has added to the Avengers mythos over the past 60 years, both on the page and on the screen. To Tom Brevoort, who drafted me onto the Avengers roster far more years ago than I care to admit. And, of course, to Jess, Charlie, and Lincoln, my own personal super team. Avengers Assemble!

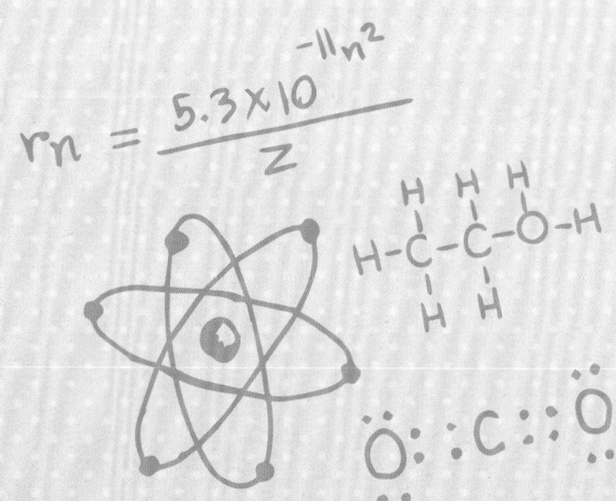

NOTES

INSIGHT
EDITIONS
San Rafael, CA 94912
www.insighteditions.com

Find us on Facebook: www.facebook.com/InsightEditions
Follow us on Twitter: @insighteditions

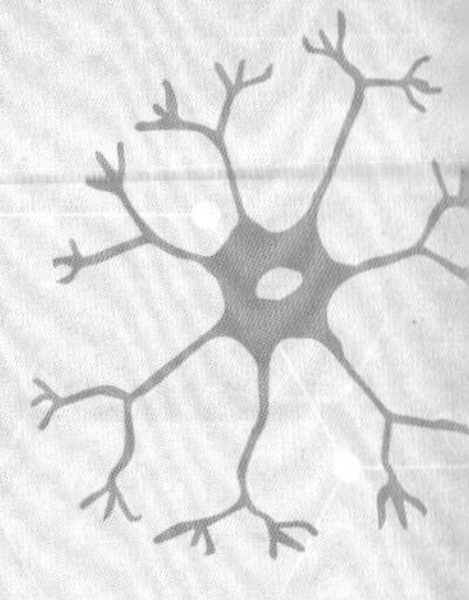

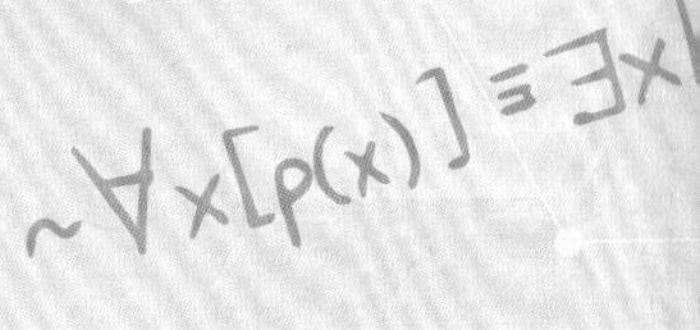

© 2022 MARVEL
© 2022 Disney

All rights reserved. Published by Insight Editions, San Rafael, California, in 2022.

No part of this book may be reproduced in any form without written permission from the publisher.

Library of Congress Cataloging-in-Publication Data available.

ISBN: 978-1-64722-547-6

Publisher: Raoul Goff
VP, Associate Publisher: Vanessa Lopez
VP, Creative Director: Chrissy Kwasnik
VP, Manufacturing: Alix Nicholaeff
Editor: Samantha Holland
Editorial Assistant: Harrison Tunggal
Managing Editor: Maria Spano
Production Associate: Deena Hashem

Photo Art Director: Judy Wiatrek Trum
Photographer: Ted Thomas
Food & Prop Stylist: Elena P. Craig
Food Styling Assistant: August Craig
Interior Design: The Book Designers

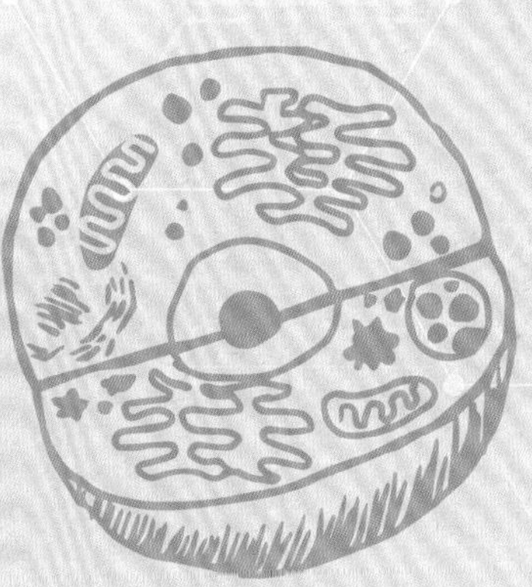

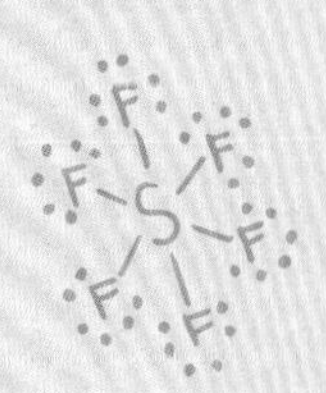

Insight Editions, in association with Roots of Peace, will plant two trees for each tree used in the manufacturing of this book. Roots of Peace is an internationally renowned humanitarian organization dedicated to eradicating land mines worldwide and converting war-torn lands into productive farms and wildlife habitats. Roots of Peace will plant two million fruit and nut trees in Afghanistan and provide farmers there with the skills and support necessary for sustainable land use.

Manufactured in China by Insight Editions

10 9 8 7 6 5 4 3 2 1